The Infinitely Gracious + *Successful* Business Owner:
How to Start, Grow, and Thrive in Your Natural Therapy or Energy Healing Business!

By Melissa Crowhurst

infinite gratitude **Natural** healer

Copyright © 2019 Infinite Gratitude t/a Natural Healer.
Last version update: March 2020.

NATURAL HEALER (logo) is trademarked under Australian Trademark No. 1991324, New Zealand Trademark No. 1114523, and U.S.A. Trademark Serial No. 88309703 (Pending).

All rights reserved. No part of this book may be reproduced by any mechanical, photographic, or electronic process, or in the form of a phonographic recording; nor may it be stored in a retrieval system, transmitted, or otherwise be copied for public or private use – other than for "fair use" as brief quotations embodied in articles and reviews – without prior written permission of the publisher.

ISBN: 9781797825625

The author of this book does not dispense medical advice or prescribe the use of any technique as a form of treatment for physical, emotional, or medical problems without the advice of a physician, either directly or indirectly. The intent of the author is only to offer information of a general nature to help you in your quest to improve your emotional, physical, and spiritual well-being.

All information provided in this book, as well as in the supplementary calculator spreadsheets, worksheets, and checklists, are general in nature and don't take into consideration your specific business or financial needs; and does not constitute financial advice in any way. In the event you use any of the information in this book for yourself or on others, the author and the publisher assume no responsibility for your actions.

Cover design: Natural Healer.
Natural Healer interior images credit: Natural Healer logo, photos of Melissa, all spreadsheets and charts. All other interior images are CC0 Public domain and/or no attribution.

Introduction 9
    Nearly three decades ago… 11
    Becoming infinitely gracious 11
Chapter 1: The keys to the kingdom 13
    Key 1. Being genuine 15
    Key 2. Being experienced 15
    Key 3. Being understanding 16
    Key 4. Being responsive 18
    Key 5. Being responsible 18
Chapter 2: The super basics 20
    Training and qualification 21
    Do I need a certificate for my inner gifts? 21
    Getting in more practice 22
    Continuing education 23
    Swimming in your lane 24
Chapter 3: Duty of care 26
    First Aid 26
    Confidentiality 27
    Appropriateness 28
Chapter 4: Pre-planning preparation 30
    From amateur to professional 31
        Pre-Planning Preparation Notepad 33
    Performance for feedback 33
    Be open and take note 34
        Feedback & Testimonial Form 35

Chapter 5: Initial Planning 36

    The checklist 37

        ☑ List out your certifications 37

        ☑ List out what services you'd like to offer 37

        ☑ Mark which services you consider yourself a pro in 37

        ☑ Understanding laws in your area in order to practice 37

        ☑ List out the products you want to sell 38

        ☑ Work from home, rent a chair, or lease a space 38

        ☑ List out the equipment, furniture, and supplies you need 38

        ☑ List out decoration you will need 38

        ☑ Are you hiring staff or taking on partners or contractors? 39

        ☑ Understand your business skillset 39

        ☑ Understand your own personality 39

        ☑ Know your financial goal 40

        ☑ Know your work-life balance goal 40

        ☑ Know your ultimate goal 40

        The Initial Planning Checklist 40

    Your next step 41

        Making the Jump Calculator 41

Chapter 6: Setting Up 43

    1. Your accountant 43

        Your business plans 44

        Your personal income 44

        Business structure 44

    Goods or service tax 45

    Employing staff 45

2. Your business name 45

    Brainstorming 45

    Research 46

    Registration 46

    Your website 46

    Trademark 46

3. Liability insurance 47

    Insurance brokers 47

4. Professional memberships 48

    Energy healing memberships 49

5. Your healing space 49

    Working from home 50

    Renting a room or chair 50

    Leasing a retail space 51

    Essential equipment 52

    A quick note about capital purchases 54

    Decoration 54

6. Hours of operation 55

    Example hours 55

    Scheduling breaks 56

7. Contact and response times 57

8. Intake forms and privacy 57

9. Pricing 58

- Service pricing 59
- Energy healing pricing 60
- Cost of goods or service 61
- Guide to pricing products 61
- Basic Profit Margin Calculator.. 63
- Payment collection 64
- The Setting Up Checklist 65

Chapter 7: Marketing your business 66
- 1. Where's the connection? 67
- 2. Your tagline and USP 70
- 3. The essentials 73
- 4. Free marketing 74
  - Local paper or newsletter 74
  - Social media 74
  - Organic search engine optimization 75
- 5. Paid marketing 76
  - Google Ads 77
  - Social media 78
  - Old school paper 78
- 6. Two effective strategies 79
  - For new or small business 79
  - For existing or larger businesses 80
  - Marketing Budget Calculator 83
- 7. Ongoing marketing 83

Chapter 8: Running your business 85

- Create processes 86
- Manage your schedule 87
- Conducting a session 88
- Client intake form 89
- Post session follow-up 89
- Responses and reviews 90
- Operating expenses 91
- Wages and related expenses 92
- Managing staff well 92
- Self-care and rest 94

Chapter 9: Growing with your business 96
- Where are you at now? 97
- Where do you want to be ultimately? 97
- Is it time to grow and expand? 98
- Preparing to grow! 99
- How do I turn things around? 103
  - Business health check 104

Chapter 10: You've got this! 109
- Giving back 109
- Thank you 110
- Infinitely Gracious Business Owner certification 111

Chapter 11: Helpful Resources 112
- Books 112
- Certificate courses and training 113
- Memberships and associations 113

Insurance 114
Accountants and book keeping 114
    Online book keeping tools 114
Business names and registration 115
Websites 115
    Other platforms in place of a website 116
    Popular social media platforms 116
Marketing tools 116
    Training 116
    Advertising platforms 117
    Email marketing platforms 117
Booking platforms 117
    Client intake form 117
Payment gateways 117
Business Coaching 118
About the author 119

Introduction

If you're reading these words right now, then I bet you're the kind of person who lives for helping others. Whether it's emotional or physical help – you thrive on seeing the positive outcomes of your efforts.

So it's little wonder why you're here with me right now: You either want to set up your first natural therapy or energy healing business, or you want to learn how to improve and grow your existing one.

I applaud you for taking these steps toward improving your situation because who wouldn't want to 'captain the ship' of their dreams, right? To earn a living from what you *love*.

Yeah, well, it's all well and good to express a few motivational words at the start of a book, but it doesn't negate the fact most businesses struggle, and even fail, in the first year.

So how does this happen to good people, who are following their hearts doing what they love?

It's because – no matter if you're performing psychic readings, giving a therapeutic massage, conducting energy healing Reiki sessions, teaching yoga, prescribing natural remedies, or something else – you will end up *getting lost* along the journey.

What I mean by that is, when people first start off, they've got excitement on their side, so they wear every single "hat" in their business. They're not just the Captain of the ship – but the first mate, the engineer, the medic, and the cook.

They were so excited to navigate those enticing uncharted waters that, as they pushed off shore, they forgot to set their inner moral "compass" to stay true to the course.

Then one day, they woke up exhausted. Their passion turned into a poorly-rewarded job of wrong turns, tireless hours, and constant compromises. They got lost.

But thankfully, now we're working together, your new business won't end up this way! And for those already in business, if my little captain and ship analogy sounds like what you're already going through, don't worry – we'll get your ship back on track!

How? Well, I'm going to give you simplified yet effective steps to follow (ones that I still use today) so you can *bypass* the ill-fate of most businesses and sling-shot yourself towards your goal!

I know that sounded a bit bold, but I've been in business for a large part of my life, so I speak with assurance from *real world experience*, not theory.

But don't let my enthusiasm make you think this journey is going to be a 'walk in the park' – a successful business can be demanding, sometimes stressful, and requires true dedication.

Nearly three decades ago…

When I turned fourteen, I was just old enough to apprentice under my mother, learning the ropes of manicuring and pedicuring. I started off by working on the weekends, then as I got older I worked after school, so by the time I graduated high school and started university, I co-owned and operated a successful beauty salon with my mother.

And that was just the start.

Fast forward nearly thirty years and here I sit with all manner of business experience under my belt: from holding 'clothing parties' to sell goods at my house; to creating a fast-paced franchise retail business with my husband; to becoming a massage therapist; to accepting the honour of being able to practice with, and teach others about, the beautiful world of energy healing.

Becoming infinitely gracious

Yet despite all those years of experience and achievement, it took self-awareness, humility, and a spiritual shift *within* to evolve myself into, what I refer to as, an *"Infinitely Gracious Business Owner"*.

What exactly is that? An *Infinitely Gracious Business Owner* is an educated and savvy entrepreneur who seamlessly blends kindness with accomplishment. Someone who understands that the ups and downs of life and business are *not* a reflection of *who they are*, but of the journey they're on.

When I started living and operating my business from that infinitely gracious and loving place, it's at that point when I finally understood:

Success has little to do with the prize you're chasing, but the prize you hold within.

Don't get me wrong, money has to abundantly flow (and in the right directions) in order to achieve your business goals; and in this book, you're going to roll up your sleeves to learn and execute real strategies to ensure you're on track for success.

But I wanted to touch on this now because, even if you just want lots of money, that big house, a flashy car, and all the glitz that goes with material success – I'm here to tell you that, while *you can* definitely achieve all those things – you aren't *really* after that *stuff*.

I'll expand more on what I mean by all this in the next chapter. For now, all I want you to keep in your mind is that you are *worthy* of - and *can* make a wonderful living from – doing what you love, in your own business.

What's more, in addition to the huge list of helpful business resources I'll provide at the end of the book, what you'll learn will ensure you never stray from the path that your inner moral compass is set to. No matter how successful you become. ☺

Okay! It's time to set sail – let's get started!

Namaste,

♥ Melissa #biglove

Chapter 1: The keys to the kingdom

What does helping others give you? Aside from a smile on your face and heart? A sense of value and worthiness.

What does having a successful business bring you? Aside from entrepreneurial respect? A sense of pride and accomplishment.

What does having excess cash flow give you? Aside from material things? A sense of relief and more time (aka. freedom).

I think we can all safely agree that, based on the above, your ideal business will produce, in addition to material success: *Value. Worthiness. Pride. Accomplishment. Relief. Freedom.*

Yet despite the wish-list you already have penned for the *one day* when your business is thriving – if we hold an emotional microscope to each and every one of those feelings above, what do we truly find? What is the actual goal you're striving for?

It's Happiness.

Essentially, it's not the money you're chasing – it's what money *frees you to do* that you're really after.

Happiness is not a job, car, house, or whatever else might be on your wish list. Happiness is a profound inward sense of significance and satisfaction in *life*.

The reason I want to highlight this is because you can have all the possessions you *think* you desire, yet not be happy. I'm sure you've known or heard of people who have all the wealth in the world, yet they suffer from depression and sadness. They're always chasing happiness.

Unfortunately, the prevailing belief in our society is that, in order for us to tap into happiness (those feeling I listed before) – we must have to *do* something. Yet we don't.

Deep down, every single one of us *already* has unrestricted access to that life goal – happiness. There is an infinite store of it within us, always. Now, this isn't a book about how to be 'happy'.

I've grazed this topic because if things get hard (and they will) or if things don't go as planned (and they might) – remember – *your happiness* remains intact.

It only seems to shatter or disappear because you *think* you *are* the result. But you're not. You are you, doing the best you can, with what you have, right now.

So make sure you draw a line in the sand right now – on your side is happiness. On the other is everything else.

Now that we've got that clear, and you're dipping into your bucket of happiness like popcorn, let's talk about my five keys to success – which, by the way, you can apply to all areas of your life for success, not only in business.

As you go through each key, embrace what feels right about them for you. And as you do, you'll see each one unlocking doors within, getting you closer to becoming an *Infinitely Gracious Business Owner!*

Key 1. Being genuine

It's no secret: everyone starts a business because they want to turn a profit. But no one should hurt others in the pursuit of it, or compromise their reputation or morals for it.

So this first key is about being genuine, honest, and sincere – within yourself, within your business, and with your customers.

Genuine *(adjective)*
truly what something is said to be; authentic;
(of a person, emotion, or action) sincere.

We all value authentic experiences, and as such, won't think twice about recommending to others whatever created that good feeling.

Yet nobody likes being lied to, especially when there's an exchange of money involved. Not only do bad experiences and insincerity travel fast and wide to wreak havoc on your business's reputation – but it taints the very core of who you are.

Stay true to your inner moral compass: **be genuine in all that you do.**

Key 2. Being experienced

When you engage someone to do something for you – and they display sureness and certainty in what they say and do – how does that make you feel? Confident and comfortable.

So as a business owner, when you speak, it should be with confidence. When you perform a service, execute it like a pro. Sure, everybody has to start somewhere – you might be just out of school – but still, achieving a minimum level of professional experience (in whatever it is you're offering) is critical for your business's success.

Experienced *(adjective)*
having gained knowledge or skill in a particular field over a period of time.

Yes, this means you have to *practice* a lot before you start charging.

It goes without saying, the more you practice something, the better you get at it. Remember, you want your clients to be confident *in* you, and comfortable *with* you – and **real experience is one of the only things that conveys proficiency without words.**

One more thing though, this key of being experienced isn't just about becoming a champion of the *actual* service you provide, but knowing how to handle emergencies, difficult clients, and other curve-balls that life *will* throw at you while you're building your business.

Experience is worth pursuing, so train, practice, and rehearse as much as you can. Both you and your clients will benefit from it.

Key 3. Being understanding

Understanding in *this* context is about comprehending your own (and others') limitations. Then from there, being able to recognise, assess, and know what to do next.

Understanding *(noun)*
an individual's perception or judgement of a situation.
sympathetic awareness or tolerance.

This doesn't mean that you should let limits stop you from achieving your goals.

Quite the contrary, understanding that you must respect physical or mental limitations (*"It's been a 18 hour day, I'm exhausted"*) and work your way through them ("*I'll go to bed now*"), with kindness to yourself ("*I did the best I could today, I'll start again tomorrow*") will enable you to maintain the focus you need to continue on the right path.

Much to our ego's surprise, we can't please everybody all the time – and – not everybody can please *us* all the time. So also being understanding of the fact that, despite best efforts, you will disappoint some people and some people will disappoint you, is **important to your inner peace**.

Please note, this isn't about 'rolling over' and just accepting everything that gets dished out in life, but about *understanding* that the circumstance is what it is – deal with it and move on.

Furthermore, being understanding of where your business is at, versus where you want it to be, will keep you from getting overly anxious. What I mean by this is that you will naturally set expectations of your business – which may or may not be realistic:

"*I want X done by this date, and I want to make X amount of money by the end of the year.*"

And if those expectations are set really tight or high, their 'incompleteness' could end up torturing you – causing angst in your life that could've been avoided.

Goals are critical in all of life, not just business, so we should have some in place. But being *understanding* that time has to pass, or that certain things have to be achieved first (or in a particular order) before your business can go from crawling to walking to sprinting – is just part and parcel of the process.

However, this doesn't give anyone license to drag their feet to get things done – there is *no room* for a procrastinator in a successful business! An *understanding* go getter – yes! But a dawdling procrastinator – no.

Key 4. Being responsive

Have you ever asked a question and never received a response? Gave a compliment or a complaint with no reply? This has probably happened to all of us, at some point or another in life, and I'm sure we can all agree - nobody likes to be forgotten or ignored.

And what does silence usually indicate to an enquiring mind? Lack of care, poor processes, unprofessionalism, and a bad attitude.

So whilst this key is short and sweet, it's an integral part of good business practice: **respond to both the good and the bad.**

Responsive *(adjective)*

reacting quickly and positively. responding readily.

in response; answering.

Ensure you set – and stick to – turn-around times for phone, email, text, messenger and mail (if anyone still uses 'snail mail' anymore) from your customers and the public.

When others see you're responsive, they gain confidence that you'll do the right thing by them.

Even if you don't know the answer right away, acknowledgement that you got the enquiry and are looking into a response, gives peace of mind.

And always responding to negative communication in a kind and diplomatic manner shows your unshakable professionalism – to everybody.

Key 5. Being responsible

The key of being responsible is what some may call a "no brainer" in business. But amazingly, there are business owners out there who say and do things (or who *don't* say or *don't* do things) without taking ownership of those actions (or inaction).

Responsible *(adjective)*
having an obligation to do something as part of one's role.
morally accountable for one's behaviour.
capable of being trusted.

It's not always easy owning up to mistakes or mishaps, but on the same token – it's one glorious reward when you can declare a success as yours. You need to be as responsible for your failings as much as you are willing to be responsible for your successes.

Remember, your business is a physical manifestation of your dreams, aspirations, and goals. So **be responsible for what you've brought into this world**.

Now with my five keys as the wind in your sails, it's time to start manoeuvring through the steps to create your business!

Chapter Recap

- No matter what business goal you have, your ultimate goal within is to achieve happiness.
- The five keys to success are being genuine, being experienced, being understanding, being responsive, and being responsible.
- Those five keys to success aren't just applicable in business, but in life, too.

Chapter 2: The super basics

Would you go pay a doctor to operate if you found they never officially graduated from school? Would you pay a plumber to fix a broken sewer if you found their entire training came from helping a friend once?

Clearly no to both. And why? Because there is *value* in education, training, practice. Not only in acquiring the skills to do the job, but also showing 'evidence' to potential clients that you *really do* know what you're doing.

But this is about natural therapies and energy healing businesses – isn't it different?

No way, not in my (literal) book!

Just because a service offering is in the natural therapy or spiritual realm, doesn't mean it can be excluded from proper training. This is a business you're going to run – so it needs to be treated as such.

So whether you're going to offer energy healing, tarot card reading, remedial massage, nutritional advice, or anything else in between – you should be officially trained and certified in your specialty. To me, that's the basic of all basics when starting a business.

For those naturally gifted healers, who might be raising and eyebrow or two over this, just hang in there. Keep reading... ☺

Training and qualification

Going through the process of obtaining professional certifications ties in nicely with 'Key 2 – Being experienced'. That and the fact most states and countries will have some sort of governing rules around you needing to be qualified or certified in order to legally work with the public.

If you're going to be a massage therapist or yoga instructor, the general public already recognises those modalities to the point where options for training and qualifications are plenty.

A quick online search will produce choices for you in full-time, part-time, and weekend classes, and even distance learning from formal training schools and universities – in a variety of fields.

Even training in energy healing (like what I offer my students with my online Reiki I, II + Master Course[1]), intuitive healing, and card readings have more routes to certification than ever before. So there is really no excuse to *not* become trained and qualified in your chosen modality.

Do I need a certificate for my inner gifts?

So what if the service you're going to provide has come to you as an inner gift (eg. clairvoyance)? The talent you possess is just part of *you* – you just know it and there is no "schooling" available; or perhaps there is schooling but it's not really what you "do".

---

[1] Information about my Reiki course here: https://naturalhealer.com.au/product/reiki-master-certification-course/

Do you still need to be trained and certified? In my opinion: yes.

In cases like this, you should look for the *next* closest field to what you're going to offer – and get trained and certified in it.

Now, don't get me wrong, this *does not* mean you aren't enough as you are! I'm not saying you need to learn something else, or how someone else does it, because you aren't capable or gifted.

But what I want you to remember is that you are starting a business! So you need to show, not just your potential clients, but possible governing bodies – that you are professional enough to have untaken valuable, structured education, practiced, and are professional enough to work with the public.

Getting in more practice

It goes without saying that you would've undergone some amount of practical training as you learned your craft. But getting in *more* practice will tip the scale from you being "good" to "amazing" at what you do!

Nothing can replace the experience you'll have, and the skill you obtain, when it's time to implement everything you learned – without your teachers or course book around.

After I became qualified to do massage (but before I took on any paying clients), I *still* practiced every single day (to my husband's great joy!) until my techniques were more natural and I came to understand my own comfort levels.

I then practiced on friends and acquaintances so I could learn how to deal with different personalities, body shapes, and sensitivities – let alone how to greet, explain, start, and end sessions.

I did the same thing *after* I became a certified Usui Reiki Master Teacher – I literally performed *hundreds and hundreds* of free energy healing sessions until I just 'knew' what my own energy was like versus others. (As a side note, doing that many sessions also taught me a lot about self-care and protection, which I'll go over later in this book!)

So if you're trying to operate a truly successful business but don't want to put in the effort to know your craft inside and out, then you'll be pushing a very large boulder uphill, for a long time – as they say.

Don't shy away from real world experience – it's the school we attend every single day. So embrace it!

Continuing education

For most qualifications which require professional memberships in order to practice with the public – like massage, chiropractors, and so on – continuing education is a *requirement* in order to keep your doors open. Even if not essential to your business, this is a great thing to do because it keeps us learning and at our best.

For example, I have to continue learning something new in the field of wellbeing, in addition to keeping my First Aid certification up to date, every year in order to maintain my Massage Association of Australia member status. The association grants me "CPE" (Continuing Professional Education[2]) credits for my new learning and apply those credits towards my membership.

So even if you're performing a modality which doesn't require you to take a new course, attend a workshop, or learn something new – I highly recommend you always continue to learn – even if it's just for your own growth.

---

[2] CPE credits are granted to MAA members who obtain my *custom* certifications (excludes my free Powerful Self-Healing course) https://naturalhealer.com.au/product-category/online-courses/

Whether you read a book, take an online course, or learn a whole new skill, as a business owner, staying abreast of new discoveries and findings, let alone new techniques, will not just give you more confidence in your field, but potentially more services to offer your clients.

Swimming in your lane

I'd like to close off my 'super basics' chapter with something called "swimming in your lane". If you've never heard of that term, let me explain a bit further.

If you've ever gone swimming in a public lap pool, you've seen the "lanes" created within it, which are divided by floating ropes. They're there so you can keep your head down while doing your laps, thus enabling you to gain and keep your momentum without worrying about bumping into someone else, or vice versa.

What would happen if you didn't pay attention to those lanes and strayed out into another? Eventually you'd collide with another swimmer, stopping you both in your tracks.

Mistakes happen, so chances are no one would be upset for too long – but what if you did it again? And again? The other swimmers would soon get upset with you, creating conflict in a shared area that should be harmonious.

So "swimming in your lane" is about knowing the boundaries of your skillset (or "lane") – and *sticking within them*. For example, if you're a massage therapist and you accidentally "adjust" someone's back while massaging – and they liked it – that doesn't mean you can now cross over to the 'Chiropractor Lane' and start adjusting people's backs.

That same principle applies to other natural therapists and energy healers, too. Many people who seek help have, or are going through, some emotional or physical distress.

Whilst there's no training required in order to be a caring and supportive person, there *is* serious training required if you start giving advice that falls into the realm of a counsellor or medical doctor.

This same concept applies when you have employees, contractors, and business partners. Everybody has their own special skills and talents, (including you!) which is why you have them on your team. When everyone respects the others' "lanes", then no collisions happen.

In short, stick to what you're trained and experienced in – "swim in your lane". If you move over into someone else's lane, you not only bump heads, but you can create problems you didn't even know were possible.

In saying this, if you find your clients want more from you than what you currently offer, consider what I said in the continuing education section just before – and take a new course or program that will train and qualify you. Alternatively, network with like-minded professionals who you can refer clients to.

So now we've got the 'super basics' covered, the next chapter is all about your Duty of Care to your clients. Which, once you embrace it, you realise how important your position as a healer and business owner truly is.

Chapter Recap

- Obtaining professional training and certification gives you the knowledge you need and gives your clients confidence in you.
- There is nothing like "real world" practice, the more you do – the better you get.
- "Swimming in your lane" reminds us to stick to providing services we're qualified and trained in.

Chapter 3: Duty of care

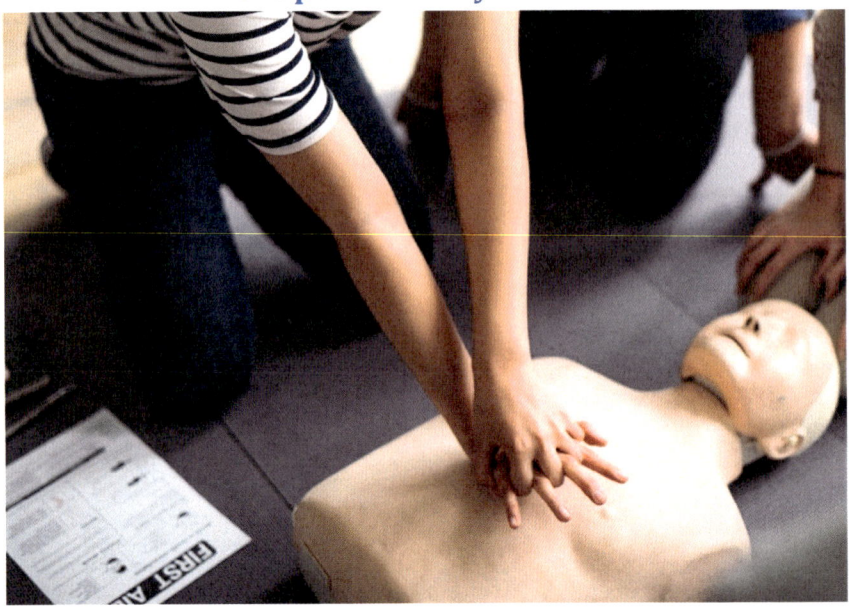

When you decide to focus on *helping others* – be that physical, emotional, or spiritual – what you do goes beyond a normal business transaction. It's no longer just an exchange of money for service, but an exchange of trust where – even if for a small moment in time – that person's welfare is your *duty*.

As such, this chapter ties in nicely with 'Key 5 – Being responsible' about your business. What is "Duty of Care"? It's essentially your legal, and even moral, obligation to ensure the safety of another.

In addition to the super basics I covered in the previous chapter, there are a couple of other components you should consider as part and parcel of your Duty of Care to your clients.

First Aid

For those who've taken any of my certificate courses, you'll know I place strong importance on learning First Aid. For practitioners already working with the public, this is a given.

But I feel that even those who are only going to work with pets, close friends or family should learn it, too.

Why? Because you are *still* placing yourself in a position of authority, and as such, take on the Duty of Care of whoever or whatever you are helping.

So whether you're at the very beginning of your business journey, or are already performing work, as part of your Duty of Care, you should learn at least the basic level of First Aid[3].

Confidentiality

The other component of your Duty of Care is the privacy and confidentiality of what you and your clients do in your sessions. As a healer, you oftentimes see your clients at their weakest and in their most vulnerable moments.

You yourself know that letting down those emotional walls to let someone else "in" to help you isn't an easy feat. That even goes with physical walls, some people carry so much burden they don't even like to be touched, so simply getting a massage is a huge leap of faith.

As such, it's critical you never breach this sacred trust by discussing your client's situation or what happened during their appointment with others. In addition to being a moral principle, it's also a business one: unless your client has given you consent to discuss their matter with a third party – do not do it.

The only exception I would ever consider is if you are stuck, and have exhausted all other options, thus seek another expert's or professional's opinion on the matter. But even in this one exception, you would still maintain strict anonymity by concealing your client's identity and identifying traits.

---

[3] Learn First aid basics here: https://bit.ly/2uvWOEJ

Appropriateness

Most healers – be they meditation guides, Reiki practitioners, chiropractors, massage therapists, or something in between – are oftentimes placed in intimate situations with clients.

And by 'intimate' I mean you may have to physically touch your client to perform the service, or be in a small space, or a dimly lit room, or simply in close proximity with them.

As such, handling yourself in an appropriate manner all the time is integral. Whether before, during, or after your session, you need to gauge – and react appropriately – to what topics are suitable given the circumstance.

I highly recommend you avoid discussing personal subjects around sex, dating, politics and religion.

I also suggest you refrain from joking around, using harsh words or slang – remember, you're the professional here. There is nothing wrong with jesting or laughing, but only when it's the right time and place. And oftentimes a client session *isn't* that time.

Remember, your client has put themselves in a position of vulnerability with you – so never discuss topics which may make them uncomfortable – even if you are passionate about it.

Also keep in mind that appropriate behaviour goes both ways. If your client is broaching unsuitable topics, you need to steer the conversation away from it. And if they do not follow your lead, you have the right to let them know (in a kind manner), that you don't find the topic appropriate – and if they do not stop – you will end the session.

Okay! Now that you know my five keys and the super basics, and we've covered your Duty of Care – it's time I teach you how to jump from being an amateur to a professional – even if you *are* new to business!

Chapter Recap

- Duty of Care is a legal and moral obligation to ensure the safety of your client.
- Learning the basics of First Aid is part of your Duty of Care.
- Client confidentiality is both a moral and business principle.
- Handling yourself appropriately at all times is paramount.

Chapter 4: Pre-planning preparation

Before we dive into the initial planning stages of the next chapter, I wanted to cover – what I consider – to be the distinguishing factor between someone who will achieve more immediate success and someone who won't. And that's with preparation.

Many people tend to rush into the set-up of a business right after they've achieved a certificate or birthed a new idea. They figure *"let's do this fast!"* because they know their skill, they've registered a business name, and off they go!

Sure, you *can* start a business like this – and it might even work. But odds are, if you are inexperienced in the world of business, you will stumble quite a lot and unnecessarily lose money (and maybe even your direction) along the way.

Inserting this pre-planning preparation phase essentially sets you up with the best chances to achieve your goal more quickly, before you take that first step. It also helps anchor you for *long term* success, too!

Note, this *is* different to getting in more practice (which I covered in the Super Basics of Chapter 2) because it's no longer about learning the *actual* skill, but how to handle things immediately before, during, and after the service you provide.

From amateur to professional

When I achieved my Usui Reiki Master Teacher status in 2014, I had already undergone quite a lot of practice. But it was mostly with my family and friends – and my sweet kitty Twinkie at the time (bless her soul).

But I didn't dive right in, although I was itching to! Why? Because I knew there would be a distinct difference between working with those within my inner circle versus complete strangers.

The familiarity of working with those you know oftentimes allows us to forget about these important questions – just to name a few:

- How will I greet them?
- When do I give them my client intake form? Before I take them into the healing room or after?
- Should I do small-talk first? Or let them complete the form first? Do I watch them complete the form, or leave them alone?
- When will I get a chance to review their form? Will I have enough time to understand what to do once I've read it?
- Should I take notes during the session? And how will I do that?
- How will I keep my client comfortable with the temperature or lighting of the room?
- What will I do if they start crying or laughing?
- What do I say when the session's done?
- What if they complain?
- How long should the post-session chat go for? Will I even do a post-session chat?

- Do I book them in for another session now? Or will I have another way to follow them up to re-book?
- At what point do I collect payment?

I realised that paying clients would expect me to have my processes 'down pat', to provide some level of results, and to have some sort of explanation or answers for them – all while maintaining their feeling of safety and certainty.

Being able to know all this stuff off the top of my head felt like a tall order, even though I had practiced so much prior to being certified. So what did I do?

Over many months, I performed *hundreds and hundreds*[4] of energy healing sessions, 100% free, for complete strangers, up close and at a distance.

That may sound epic (and to some degree it was!), but I feel this preparation was the point of difference I needed. It showed me how to be a true business professional *as well* as an effective energy healer.

Remember, these sessions weren't about 'practicing' the craft anymore, but learning how to juggle all the components of the session as well as the client's expectations.

This was pre-planning *preparation* I felt I needed before I could officially start charging for my energy healing services.

---

[4] I do *not* recommend you exert this level of effort if you are very inexperienced with energy healing and/or aren't well versed in protecting and disconnecting with energy work. You must also gauge your own well-being and always ensure you honour and respect *your mind, body, and spirit*.

Pre-Planning Preparation Notepad

To make this step a bit easier, and to help you solidify your ideas, use my "Pre-Planning Preparation Notepad" (PDF) here: https://bit.ly/2SV3gBb

Performance for feedback

Whilst I enjoyed all those free sessions immensely, I did have two upfront requests from those who allowed me to work with them in my 'business preparation' phase and that was:

1. Please give me honest feedback – where could I have improved in the process?
   and
2. Please provide me with a testimonial – what did you think I did really good?

Because I already had clientele as a working massage therapist, I didn't actually ask anyone what they would pay for the service, as I planned to offer it as an "add-on" at a small cost.

My energy healing work did eventually morph into its own service, and at that point I then provided it at the same price as my massages.

But in saying all this, if I *didn't* have clients already, or if the service would be completely foreign to my clientele, I would have added a third request from those free sessions:

3. Please tell me what you thought the session was worth?

Keep in mind that if you're brand new to this and don't have an existing clientele to work with – or are perhaps a little unsure – 'tagging' along with another healer or at an appropriate event is a great way to get yourself in front of those you don't already know.

For example, there may be organisations or groups who are open to you offering your service to their members for free; or perhaps you know someone who runs a market stall or small business, or know of a small party or function that's coming up – all of which are great avenues for you to 'perform for feedback'.

Be open and take note

Clearly you will need to be open and ready for feedback – irrespective of if you're providing the service for free or at a price. Keep your mind and heart open as you will likely get ideas or tips on how to improve the customer experience or how you do something.

But at the same time, please realise that when you ask for feedback, some of it may challenge your ego!

Everybody experiences life in their own way, so whilst you may have done the best you could – it might not have 'rocked' someone's world – and *that's okay*.

Constructive or negative feedback helps you refine your process – *if* you let it be the fuel for you to level up with. On the other hand, if you take it too personally, it will drag you down – which won't help you or the client. So just keep this in mind, as a *service provider,* you've put yourself 'out there' - so be open and accept what others have to say – both the good and bad.

And just remember, acceptance doesn't mean you agree with it or are going to do whatever the person said. Acceptance is the grace you display in receiving someone's valid perception of what they experienced with you – even if you don't agree.

This process not only helps you refine the steps of your actual service, but also gives you the chance to take note of those testimonials for future use. So collect, save, and use those testimonials!

This way you can display the honest experience from those who worked with you in a professional way to your brochures, website or socials. These true testimonials may give potential clients, who could be 'sitting on the fence', that little nudge they needed to contact you.

Feedback & Testimonial Form

I've created a feedback and testimonial form you can use for this step! The PDF version is here: https://bit.ly/2IwdHWP but if you want to add your own logo or change any of the questions, the Excel spreadsheet version is here: https://bit.ly/2GJO0k6

Okay! So all of the groundwork we've done to this point means that you're now in the *best position* to actually start planning your business, which we'll dive into in the next chapter!

An important note to current business owners!

Don't skip the upcoming planning section. Even if you've 'ticked' all the boxes up to this point, the next chapter will allow you to cross-check if you are on track with your business goals – and perhaps even super-charge you towards them!

Chapter Recap

- Preparing for business is about practicing your service with strangers to gain a better understanding of how you can improve the process.
- Instead of charging a fee for this step, ask for feedback, a testimonial, and what the person *would* pay if you were to charge.
- Listening and taking on-board constructive or negative feedback is how you grow as a person, as a healer, and a business.
- Collect, save, and use the testimonials.

Chapter 5: Initial Planning

There are a million ways to get from point A (where you are now) to point B (your business's success). The pathways could be on the ground, in the air, meandering, zig-zagging, boomeranging, and full of continuous delays and lay-overs.

Yet out of all those options, there's likely to be a handful – if not *the one* – that is the *most efficient* route to point B.

But how will you know that unless you plan?

Please note that the initial planning isn't just about what's going to be on your menu of services, or what your operating hours will be, but also about what you want to do long term with your business. That and it will ensure you've documented what your actual goals are – so you never lose sight of them – and stay on course!

So take your time with this – it's your future we're planning here!

The checklist

This is a comprehensive checklist, but be mindful that not everything on it will be applicable to you; yet also note there could be things you need to *add* to the checklist.

If you flicked ahead, you might be thinking *"Eeek! There's a lot on this checklist!"* but don't worry, I provide a condensed version of it in PDF format (at the end of this section) so you can print it out for easier use and reference.

☑ List out your certifications
So what are the exact things you're certified in? These certifications give you the ability to provide *that* service in your business.

☑ List out what services you'd like to offer
When doing this, take note of any services you've listed which your certifications *do not* cover. This either means you need to undergo training to get that qualification, or find someone who has it to work with or for you.

☑ Mark which services you consider yourself a pro in
Any services which you don't consider yourself a 'pro' with, go back to the previous chapter and look to get in as much 'performance for feedback' practice as you can.

☑ Understanding laws in your area in order to practice
Depending on where you live, there may be certain laws regulating services offered to the public. For example, some States in the U.S.A. require Reiki Practitioners to be a Licensed Massage Therapist in order to practice.

Furthermore, it's very important you **do not** make any claims that you can 'cure' a disease or illness. The strictness of this will vary depending on where you're located in the world.

As an example: in the U.S.A., the American Medical Association controls certain terms, such as "diagnose", "prescribe", "recommend" and "advise" – when used in a healing capacity – whereby those words can only be used by licensed medical doctors. That means using those terms are *illegal* if you're practicing in the U.S.A. or its territories, unless you're legally allowed to do so.

If you're unsure, contact the business department of your local council or governing body to discuss what you plan to do, and they'll point you in the right direction to understand what requirements you must meet in order to work with the public. This may include things like business name, association memberships, insurance and so on – which I'll cover a bit more in the next chapter.

☑ List out the products you want to sell
It could be a good idea to sell products as a great 'add-on' to your service. As you list these out, take note of who the suppliers are so you know who to contact in the near future.

☑ Work from home, rent a chair, or lease a space
Clearly there are associated costs with renting a room or chair and leasing a commercial space. So many healers start by working from home or becoming an employee of another business. It's important you think about where you're at in your life and pick the right space for you to take these first steps in.

☑ List out the equipment, furniture, and supplies you need
This could be as basic as a massage table, chairs, stereo, and towels – to larger scale items like a reception desk, cash register, tools, and machinery.

☑ List out decoration you will need
Not many people like a cold, sterile environment when in a healing situation, so look around the space you're going to use and decide if it needs to be lightened up, more private, more inspirational, and so on.

☑ Are you hiring staff or taking on partners or contractors?

Depending on where you're at in your business journey, it may be beneficial to get some help if you're busy, or to help "round out" your service offering.

If you're hiring staff, you need to ensure you understand your obligations and duties as an 'employer' – I'll go over this a bit more in the next chapter. If you've rented a space or have a lot of room, you could possibly sub-lease to another healer to help you off-set your costs.

Of course, you will need to ensure your land-lord allows this, so check with them first.

☑ Understand your business skillset

Are you business-minded? Good with numbers? Good with money? Good with marketing? It's important to remember that whilst it's possible to be jack or jill of all trades, being that way makes it hard to be a master in anything.

So if you need to hire a book keeper to help you with your finances – even if just an hour here and there – do it if you can. Get help from someone who understand how to create good advertisements if that's not something you're brilliant in.

Understand what you will need help with and start noting down who those other experts are who will become part of your business back-bone.

☑ Understand your own personality

Are you the best person to handle problems? Complaints? Staff? Not everybody is good at managing people, as there's a delicate balance between being respected and authoritative (as opposed to liked and bossy).

So if you always get 'walked over' or staff tend to argue with you a lot –

perhaps managing people isn't your forte. Understanding your personality in conjunction with management and difficult situations is important – take note of this as it forms the foundations of your business.

☑ Know your financial goal
What do you need to earn (less your expenses) to achieve your goal. Don't be shy here, this is the planning phase and unless you plan for your future, it will remain hazy.

Work out what you want to "take home" in earnings (after all your expenses are paid) so you know the number you're aiming for. This is a goal – not the reality right now – but a goal.

☑ Know your work-life balance goal
This is different to your financial goal, this is all about your stress to relaxation ratio. How many hours do you want to work in a day? How many days do you want to work in a week? How much time off do you want to have each year?

Is this an 'on the side', part-time, or full-time career move? Again, remember this is a *goal* – not what's happening right now.

☑ Know your ultimate goal
This varies again from the previous two goals because it's what you *ultimately* want from your business in the long term. Do you want to grow it nationally or internationally? Do you want to end up selling it, or franchising it, one day? Is it a legacy for your children? Is it your contribution to society or the world?

Let your *real dreams* bubble up here! If you don't let those dreams become vivid in your mind and put pen to paper, it's much harder to achieve it.

The Initial Planning Checklist
To make this process much easier, I've turned these items into a

checklist (PDF) that you can download and work from: https://bit.ly/2SYCd7Y

Your next step

Now that you've gone through the initial planning checklist, you might feel a bit overwhelmed – and I get that! As such, let's just focus on your next step.

For those already in business, go back through the initial planning checklist and ensure you work on the *next highest priority* item. You'll know which one that is by downloading and completing the checklist from the previous section in this chapter. But also keep reading – I think you'll also benefit from what I'm going to provide to first-timers, too!

For those new to business or who are going to be doing this "on the side" until they can earn enough to do it full-time, I've created a very simple, yet oftentimes missed, process that will allow you to start realising your dreams:

1. Work out how much money you earn per day at your current job. This is the "gross" amount before taxes or anything is taken out.
2. Once you have that number, set that as your financial goal for your side-business at the moment. Yes, just that *one* number.

I've asked you to do this because this allows you to know what your side-business needs to make to replace a single day of work at your normal job. Naturally, the more your side-business earns, the more days you can see you'll be able to replace.

But, before you jump ship – make sure your business can generate this money in a steady and ongoing manner. By doing this you'll be sure to reduce the financial pressure most people put themselves under when going 'solo'.

Making the Jump Calculator

To make it easier for you – I've created a little calculator (XLS fie) to help you work through this phase. It's quite exciting to keep it up to date as you'll soon see yourself getting closer and closer to your goals!

Use this to help you plan 'making the jump' from employee to business owner: https://bit.ly/2SqQh4V

Once your checklist is complete and you've worked out what you need to make the jump, it's time to start getting *really* serious about your business by setting it up!

Chapter Recap

- The Planning Checklist allows you to see what areas you're strong in, and where you need help.
- The Planning Checklist helps create a path to your future success, so it's important to go through it fully – and refer to it often!
- The Making the Jump calculator allows you to create short-term achievable goals for your business – so you can see it growing!

Chapter 6: Setting Up

By now you surely understand that, if done the right way, your business can and will sustain you for the 'long haul'. With all the amazing knowledge and skill you've managed to stuff under your belt – I bet you are *so ready* for this moment!

Take a few deep breaths and **take your time** with this. I cover as much as I possibly can in this section and it won't benefit you to skim the surface if you really want to have the depth and breadth of understanding you need as a successful business owner for the long term.

So without further ado, let's set up that wonderful business of yours!

1. Your accountant

Even if you're first step is to just start doing a little work "on the side" of your day job, it's really important that you reach out to your accountant for some help and advice on how that extra (or 'hobby') money will impact your personal income and taxation.

Keep in mind that there is a distinct difference between the good ol' family accountant who's simply does your income tax returns each year and a solid business accountant.

Your current accountant may, or may not, be proficient working with business structures and taxation – so it's very important to ask how much experience they have in working with your type of business.

I stress this now because as your business grows – if you don't consider the right business structure and tax implications early on, it could cost you down the track. So take that little bit of time to get this set up right, from the beginning.

Here are a few topics to start the discussion with your accountant:

Your business plans
Remember the initial planning checklist from the previous chapter? Well that's going to come in really handy now! Take that in to discuss the relevant topics with your accountant. This will give them great insight which will help them *help you*.

Your personal income
You'll then want to discuss how your business venture may impact your personal taxation and work out with them the best way to organise this. Remember, your accountant is trained to help you make the most out of your situation, so be sure to utilise their expertise!

Business structure
Depending on your situation, once your accountant knows your plans, they'll be able to assess what sort of business structure is good for you now and for the long term.

For some it could be as simple as just "trading" under your own personal name as an independent contractor, while for others setting up a full-blown company could be better. But depending on where you live, the process of setting up the right structure *could* be complicated, so it's wise to get professional help on this one.

Goods or service tax
You also need to discuss your legal obligations to collect and pay sales tax on any goods and services you're providing. There's a good chance you might have to complete additional registrations (beyond just a business name registration) to obtain specific business identification numbers for this.

This step will vary widely from county, to state, to country – so make sure you cover this topic with your accountant!

Employing staff
By the time you get to this topic with your accountant, they'll likely be able to easily advise what steps you need to take to employ staff. Based on your current situation and goals, you'll discuss whether you just need contractors or 'casual' staff, or perhaps permanent part- or full-time staff.

Your discussion should also include covering off what you're legally liable for as an employer. This can encompass everything from minimum pay rates to extra benefits, and more.

2. Your business name
A lot of small businesses will start using a business name that they like without doing any sort of research first. Sure, it might be something you love and adore and have used for some time. But if someone else registered or trademarked it before you – you will likely have to go through the costly re-branding process, if not a lawsuit.

Brainstorming
Depending on the type of goods or services you're providing, ensuring you select a business name that *reflects* that core offering is really important. For example, if you teach yoga, try and get the term "yoga" in your business name.

Alternatively, if you want to use a business name that doesn't have your offering in it – that's fine too – just keep in mind that the more obscure the name is to the general public, the more work you'll need to do in explaining what it is that you do.

In saying this, unique business names can be catchy and memorable – so if you go with this option, make sure you create a "tagline" that goes with it. I'll cover taglines a bit more in the upcoming marketing section of the book.

Research

Your local government will have a way for you to research if the business name you want is available to register and use. Don't skip this part! Do your research first before you get too attached the business name you've chosen!

Registration

Also, since you would've chatted with your accountant by this point, you'll know whether you just need to register a business name to 'trade' under or if you need to register a business name *and* set up a company.

The process of business registration will vary widely from county, to state, to country – so make sure you ask questions about how to best do it, or perhaps get your accountant to do it for you!

Your website

In our growing digital world, the chances are you'll need to set up a website – even if just basic so more people can find you. Most major providers (I'll list out some for you in the resources section at the end of the book) can make the process of registering and setting up a website very easy.

So even if you aren't ready to launch your site just yet, at least claim the URL (also known as a "domain name") of your business now (e.g. https://naturalhealer.com.au) so it's secure for your future use.

Trademark

A trademark is basically a symbol, or a word or words, which is legally registered to represent a company, product or services. If you've ever seen the symbol ™ next to a name or logo, it means that name or logo is trademarked and cannot be used by anyone else.

If you're just starting out, getting your business name or logo trademarked might not be necessary. However, as your business grows – you may want to ensure that others don't (purposely or inadvertently) use or copy your business name or logo.

You don't want potential clients getting confused over which company is "really" you, or perhaps have another business taint your reputation since they have the same business name as you.

The process of getting a trademark involves using an experienced Trademark Lawyer and can be costly. So if you're ready for this step, make sure you engage a reputable legal team.

3. Liability insurance

When referring to business, getting insurance coverage is all about protecting your business from the risk of "liability" to pay for costs related to some form of negligence. Hence the term, liability insurance. Essentially, this type of insurance makes sure that you're protected in the uncommon event a lawsuit or legal claim is made against your business.

Insurance brokers

Getting insurance *can* be complicated. Why? Because the requirements for running a business vary so widely from county, to state, to country – which can make the process of getting adequate insurance to cover that business less cut-and-dry.

For example, some states in the USA require additional qualifications for energy healing Reiki practitioners to actually practice and get insurance. So if you don't know the requirements, you could end up in a bit of a pickle down the track!

You don't want to *think* you're covered just to end up finding out later that you're *not,* just because you missed a step or didn't know how to set it up right from the start.

But don't worry! I don't mean to get all heavy and serious here! I just want to make sure you understand the importance of getting this step 100% correct from the start; and you can do that by simply using a professional insurance service.

As such, I highly suggest you use an experienced insurance brokerage firm[5] so you get the right coverage for your situation. To help you with this important step, I'll provide recommendations in the resources section at the end of this book.

4. Professional memberships

Whilst most natural healing modalities have the same *fundamentals* (helping others heal in the most natural way possible), as you know by now, the requirements to practice with the public will vary depending on *what* you're offering and *where* you're going to offer it.

As such, you may - or may not - have an obligation to maintain some sort of professional membership in order to practice your craft.

For example, as a massage therapist here in Victoria, Australia, I have to maintain my membership with the Massage Association of Australia (MAA) in order for me to keep my associated insurance coverage in place. And part of the requirement of my MAA membership is that I continue to educate myself in my field, as well as keep my First Aid qualification up to date.

---

[5] For those in the USA, my preferred partner covers all 50 states with premiums from as little as USD$96/year: http://bit.ly/2NdxUD9

Other than asking your school or trainer, another easy way to find out if you *need* to maintain a professional membership within your field is to contact a prospective insurance provider to see what *they* require in order to approve your liability insurance.

Energy healing memberships

For many intuitive healers and energy healers, the ability to regulate what memberships are required for natural and innate healing gifts isn't as straight-cut as it is for chiropractors, massage therapists, and so forth.

In saying this, there are a lot of natural and energy healing associations and membership organisations that healers can join, like my Natural Healer Society. Just keep in mind that their requirements will vary greatly – so you'll just need to do your own due diligence on what you're looking for out of an organisation and if that particular one will suit your needs.

But even if you *don't* have to become a member of an association, it's still good business practice to be a part of one.

Why? Because when your client sees that you prescribe to a professional code of conduct, there is a subconscious 'trust' that gets exchanged between you and them. They will naturally have more confidence in what you're doing.

5. Your healing space

Now that we've pushed through some of the 'heavier' components of your business set up, it's now time to think about your healing space! It's really important to foster a space that will encourage your client to relax and thrive, in addition to its location. So let's talk through some of the considerations of your healing space.

First and foremost, you need to work out if you're going to offer your services from home, rent a room or chair in another business location, or lease out a retail space of your own.

Clearly each one of these options will have varying commitments, cost and marketing factors, so it's important to consider your situation and needs in addition to *where* you think your potential clients are.

Working from home

If you decide to work from home, try to make it where your clients don't have to navigate through too much of your own personal areas to get to your healing space. Whilst your home set up might not allow total separation, just have a good think about how you can keep your business as separate as possible from your personal living quarters.

For example, strategically place a decorative divider so as your client heads down the hallway, the view of your living area is blocked from them.

You'll also want your healing space to be accessible, ideally, very easily and on the peripheral of your home. For example, an office near the front door, or maybe in a converted garage.

When I first started doing massages, I lived in a four-story townhouse and the only spare room I had was all the way at the top! Not ideal for sure, but the good thing was that the stair way was at the front of the house. That meant if I just closed the doors to my personal rooms before I started my work day, my clients never saw my "personal" areas.

- **Pros:** Little to no overheads; no commute; full personalisation of your healing space.
- **Cons:** People coming to your home; less 'divide' between work and play; harder to get new clients who aren't referrals.

Renting a room or chair

This is a great option for those who don't want to lease a space and for those who don't or can't work from home. Another bonus of renting a room or chair in an existing business is that you can reach new clients that are already frequenting that location.

A lot of businesses are happy to get qualified practitioners to rent spaces from them as it adds to their service list in addition to giving them some extra revenue (by way of your rent), too!

Because my healing room was on the fourth floor of my townhouse, I was also "on the books" at a nearby healing centre. This meant I could use their massage room for my clients who couldn't quite make it up my staircase, as well as offer sessions to their clientele, too. I simply paid a "room fee" each time I completed a session.

It's really a win-win for both the healer and the other business, and is a natural progression if you want to start branching out if working from home isn't generating the income you want or need.

To get started with this, just research your local beauty salons, spas, or healing centres, and ask them if they have rooms or chairs to rent. Based on that, you can assess whether that space is good for you.

- **Pros:** You can increase your clientele and therefore your revenue; it costs less than fully leasing; create relationships with others who work in the space.
- **Cons:** Actual 'hard' costs you must pay in rent; less personalisation over your healing space; some level of commute.

Leasing a retail space

This option is clearly for those healers who either *need* a public location, or who are ready for that next step in growth!

For example, if your yoga classes are getting too big to continue to hold in your back yard, and you have clients requesting more services, then leasing an appropriate retail space could be the right next step for you.

Not only does having your own retail premises give you back the ability to fully personalise the space the way you want, but it gives you the opportunity to expand the service offering you can provide.

What's more, you'll have more chances of getting "walk by" or "walk in" traffic – so that's people who just happened to see your storefront and come in to use you. You can also consider renting out a room or chair to other healers (but that's subject to your lease, so please discuss that with your landlord first), or get independent contractors in to work with you.

When my mother and I opened our beauty salon together, our service list was able to double because we had an aesthetician come in to do facials and waxing as well as a massage therapist. This meant more options for our clients and more revenue for us – yet we didn't have to learn those skills ourselves.

In saying this though, proceeding with commercial leases isn't 'light weight' by any means. Oftentimes the leases are longer in duration, quite costly, and come with an array of other expenses (electricity, water, sewerage or garbage collection, and other fees) – all of which you have to factor into your business goals, and your long term goals.

If you're teetering back and forth on whether or not this is the right option for you – go back and review your financial, work-life balance, and ultimate goals in the initial planning chapter. This will help keep you on course with your goals. That and have a chat with your accountant, too. They add a great 'level-headed' perspective for you to consider in your decision making process.

- **Pros:** Full control over the space; ability to bring in other contractors and healers; greater reach to a wider public audience; possible higher turnover.
- **Cons:** Full financial responsibility for the lease and outgoings (expenses you're liable for in the operation of the premises, like

a percentage of property tax, water, electricity and so on); juggling other staff or contractor schedules and personalities; higher expenses.

Essential equipment

Clearly this part of setting up your business is going to revolve quite tightly around what your actual natural therapy or healing business is. In saying this, there are some fundamental pieces of equipment that I think *most* businesses in this field should have.

Of course, there may be more (or less) things you need for your session that what I've listed here, but this should at least help you get started with what you need to open your healing space to clients:

- **Clipboard and pen** – for your client to easily complete their intake form, and for you to then take notes on.
- **Folder or binder** (and hole punch or plastic sleeves) – for easy storage and reference of your intake forms.
- **Comfortable seating** – for your client, whether for the whole session or for before they begin their session with you.
- **Comfortable mat or massage table** – for your client, if you require them to lay down at any time, or to help evoke relaxation for your treatment.
- **A seat or stool on wheels** – for you so it's easier to move around your client while remaining seated and comfortable.
- **Stereo and music** – for an enhanced healing atmosphere, remember to put the music on repeat or loop so it continues throughout the whole session.
- **Soft lighting with lamps** – for a more calming and relaxed environment, so you can turn off the main overhead lights.
- **Pillow** – for your client's head comfort if lying down, or to support their lower back while sitting. Remember to get a pillow protector and cover too, so you can remove and wash it after each client.

- **Blankets or towels** – for your client's warmth, sense of security or for privacy if lying down.
- **Tissues** – for any unexpected coughs, sneezes, or tears present themselves during the session.
- **Jug of fresh clean water and glasses** – for when you need to clear a 'frog' in the throat to help cleanse toxins after a session.
- **Hand sanitiser** – for you to use before you start your session on your client.
- **Anti-bacterial wipes** – for post-session clean-up of your massage bed or chair.

A quick note about capital purchases

Whilst I'm not an accountant, I'd like to at least make you aware of what "capital purchases" are because, as a professional business owner, it's good to know when you purchase something that adds value to your business.

Many of the items and equipment you need to buy when first starting your business will be considered "capital purchases" – which are items that are considered an "asset".

For example, your massage table, a reception desk, and even a work vehicle are considered capital purchases. Yet a box of tissues or a subscription to accounting software aren't capital purchases.

If you want more clarity around what capital purchases are and aren't for your situation, please chat with your accountant.

Decoration

It goes without saying that your healing space should be warm, welcoming and loving – because those are the feelings which your clients need to experience in order to relax and truly benefit from your session.

So when decorating your healing space, please remember to infuse the area with strategic colours and visuals which will evoke the kind of response you want your client to experience.

For example, if you lead meditation groups – using a lot of red colours and fast-tempo music isn't likely to lead your clients to a place of calm and peace. Yet hues of soft blue and green, with gentle sounds of the ocean or soft music will probably help your session be more successful.

Whilst it's very tempting to decorate with all the wonderful pieces I've collected over the years, I still choose to keep my healing area simple, with just a comfy couch, massage table, candles, a painting of flowers, and stereo.

6. Hours of operation

It's very easy when you first start out, to take every and all client enquiries that you can so you get that experience you need. But even so, you do need to set some boundaries around when you work – and when you rest.

Take some time now to work out the best hours for you – keeping in mind that you need to also cater to when your clients are most likely going to want to book.

Remember, most people work Monday to Friday 9am – 5pm, so if you want to ensure you 'lower the hurdle' for clients to come see you, think about offering some after-5pm appointments on certain nights, and maybe open up a slot or two on the weekend.

Example hours

When I first started offering massage, I had to play around a bit with what hours best suited my physical stamina, my life, and my clients' needs. But it didn't take long before I found my ideal hours, which are below:

- Monday – Off
- Tuesday – 12pm to 8pm

- Wednesday 10am – 6pm
- Thursday – 12pm – 8pm
- Friday 10am – 7pm
- Saturday 10am – 12 noon
- Sunday - Off

Of course, I was flexible, so if someone needed to see me a little earlier or later, I would accommodate if I could. Setting these hours didn't just give my business its hours of operation, but enabled me to plan things in my life, so I could get some rest and 'playtime', too.

Scheduling breaks

Based on what you do, your efforts may or may not be labour intensive; however, almost any service-based offering can end up being emotionally draining.

So when scheduling your clients, especially if you're starting to get really busy – give yourself *at least* 15-minutes (ideally 30-minutes) in between sessions so you can rest.

You'll be amazed at how a quick sit down – close your eyes and breathe deeply – and glass of water can recharge you. This break is really two-fold in its effect: it gives you the rest you need *and* allows you to put forth your best effort for the next client.

If you work longer days, remember to respect your body and take a decent 60-minute lunch or tea break. Without you – there is no business. So don't ever compromise the sacredness of your *Spiritual House*[6].

---

[6] I like to refer to our bodies as 'Spiritual Houses', you can read more about my viewpoint at my blog: https://naturalhealer.com.au/2014/11/spiritual-house/

7. Contact and response times

This set up step echoes back to 'Key 4 – Being Responsive'. You need to establish what modes of contact your clients will get in touch with you to book, and what sort of time-frames you'll put on responses, reminders, and cancellations.

The most common contact methods would be phone and email. But nowadays there are appointment setting programs and social platforms to consider, too.

Just be mindful that whatever method you publish for potential clients to book with you – that how long you take to respond could be the *first impression* you make on them – so make it a good one.

So this means your hours of operation should be stated on your website, your premises, and on your voicemail; as well as your typical response time to any messages received or left.

If you have stationary (like brochures) and business cards, it's a good idea to pop that same information on them, too.

8. Intake forms and privacy

Whether you need to know a lot of information about your client – or not, you should always have a client intake form for them to complete.

This gives you the opportunity to obtain your client's full contact details, learn about injuries or concerns, understand what their expectations or goals for the session are, as well as have them sign a disclaimer or waver about the extent or limitations of your treatment, and opt-in to future marketing or promotions you may have in future. (We'll talk about marketing in the next chapter!)

In saying this, whenever you gather personal information about another person – just remember what I taught you back in the 'Duty of Care' chapter. You are in a position of authority, and as such, are privy to sensitive information. So honour the trust your client has shown you and keep what you learn about them, and what happens during the session, private and confidential.

If you don't have one already, here's a copy of my energy healing client intake form that you can use or take inspiration from:
https://bit.ly/2SgjuQe

9. Pricing

I get asked, *"What should I charge?"* quite a lot from my students and most of the time I respond with: *"What your clients are willing to pay."* Now this doesn't mean you should *undercharge* or just price something based on someone else's opinion – but what I *do* mean is that you need to *listen* to your clients when working out what to charge.

If you've just priced your service without any research into your marketplace – you will either: not make enough money to cover your costs, or you won't get a lot of bookings.

If you continuously look at your schedule and there's cobwebs on it – it *may* be something to do with how you've priced your service. It might not be, but you should be willing to look into it as a possibility.

For example, I have a 'friend of a friend' sort of acquaintance who is spiritually gifted and can do readings. She was told by a "successful business person" that she should charge at least AU$100 for a session. Yet after many months, she had no paid bookings.

Now whilst I don't think there's anything technically amiss with that pricing, where I think this amazing woman went wrong was that she was pricing her service way outside the "going rate" for readings by *unknown* intuitives. If she had lots of testimonials and a solid clientele who referred others to her, then the chances are that her AU$100 rate would've been very reasonable.

But since she was *brand new* to offering her gifts to the public (she didn't have any clients on the books outside of her family and friends) and no one knew her talents – AU$100 was out of reach the her marketplace and it would've been seen as a bit of a 'gamble' to most people.

When I suggested she look to change her pricing to match the "going rate" that other tarot and intuitive reading businesses charged (which was about half what she was charging), she refused – and that's okay. But unfortunately, her business never took off.

Let me get this straight though, even if she *did* lower her pricing to match her competitors, her business still may not have flourished. As you know by now, there are my 'Five Keys to the Kingdom', in addition to a whole lot of other business considerations, that make for a successful business.

What I'm highlighting here is that she refused to "meet the market" – that's offering a needed service at a price clients are willing to pay. And because of that she *never gave her business a chance*. She priced herself "out" of the market before she even got started.

So let's make sure you give your business every possible chance of getting off the starting block with getting your pricing right!

Service pricing

For services like chiropractic adjustments or massage therapy, there's enough competition out there to do research around in order to see what the "going rate" is.

For example, when I first started doing massage here in Australia back in 2012, a 60-minute massage session was about AU$60 - $70, give or take. Since I was new to the 'massage market', I initially offered my sessions way *under* that amount – at an incredibly low AU$50.

I never planned on keeping the pricing that low, but I strategically offered that 'opening' price just to get clients in. As you can imagine, I got booked up so quickly that it didn't take long before I increased my price to AU$70. (I'll go over this strategy a bit more in the upcoming marketing chapter, so hang tight!)

And because I increased the price incrementally over several months, (so not right away in one go), none of my clients were bothered by it. By then they knew how much I put into my services – and some of them even paid me *more* than my price because they felt it was worth more than what I charged!

So it's best that you do a bit of research around what others are charging for the service you plan on offering – and if applicable, look in your local areas first – so when you price, you can model that "going rate".

Then after that, when you're busy and booked out, you can review your pricing if necessary.

Energy healing pricing

Because energy healing is so very personal, and results vary quite a lot depending on the client's willingness and openness, it might not be as easy to find "going rates" for what you offer.

Add to that, because energy healing can be just as *good for the healer* as it is for the client, some practitioners work for free or for donations only.

So if you're finding it hard to set a price, then hark back to what you did for your 'Performance for feedback' (back in Chapter 4). Remember when you practiced "for real" like a business but instead of charging, your payment was feedback?

That information will now come incredibly handy! And remember, what you decide to set your price as now isn't forever. Price your services in a way where you feel rewarded, but also in a way that will allow the most people to be able to benefit from what you do.

For example, my clients were only used to my massage service and pricing – so when I decided to add Reiki energy healing into the mix, I only charged an additional AU$15 for 15-minutes of energy healing. For my clients, it was a small price to try out something new, so most of them took the opportunity to experience it!

Then over time, as my clients started feeling the positive shifts from my energy healing "add on" – they started wanting to do just those types of sessions, too.

Because these sessions were less "labour intensive" as my massages, I decided to charge AU$50 for a 60-minute session. The session itself was only about 30-minutes in duration, but I discussed my client's emotional needs before the session, then had a post-session chat afterward – so overall it ended up being an hour in total.

So between doing research about what the "going rate" is for services that are like yours, or at least in your industry, and reviewing your 'Performance for feedback' notes – you should have a good idea of where to get started with your pricing.

Cost of goods or service

As you know, I'm not an accountant so won't go into great detail about "cost of goods". But again, I want to give you some basic exposure to the term and what it is. The cost of goods is the sum total of what it cost you to directly make a product or to perform a service each time you do it.

For example, to make a candle – you need a jar, a wick, wax, and maybe a label for the jar. The cost of each of those items combined equates to your cost of goods. If you need massage oil to perform massages, that cost would need to be considered when costing your service.

However, cost of goods *doesn't* normally include things like wages, rent, or the chair you sat on to make the candle. Those things are separate and I'll quickly touch on them later in the book. But if you need more clarity around this now, please chat with your accountant.

Guide to pricing products

If you have the desire and room to hold stock, selling products to complement your service is a great idea. For example, if you teach yoga – giving your clients the option to purchase mats, socks, and other gear could be a great little 'extra' source of income for you.

In saying this though, if you're new to selling products, you need to take a few things into consideration so you don't *lose* money on the sale.

Generally someone who sells a product to the public (and let's assume that's you) is referred to as a retailer. The business who supplies the you (the retailer) with said products is called a wholesaler, or wholesale supplier.

Wholesalers will have a price they sell a product to you for, and sometimes they may have a "Recommended Retail Price" (RRP) you should then on-sell that product for.

For example, let's say you decide to sell soy candles. You've found a wholesale supplier who lets you purchase them at $10 each, plus tax, and you must buy 6 at a time.

You must also pay for shipping to your home, which is expensive because they're heavy, so it's another $18, plus tax. The wholesaler says you should sell the candles at a RRP of $30 each, plus tax.

So let's work out what the actual cost of the item is to see if it's worthwhile selling them:

- $10 wholesale price, per candle
- Plus another $1 (10% tax the supplier charges you)
- Plus another $3 (that's the $18 shipping divided by 6 candles)
- Plus another $0.30 (10% tax on the shipping)

When you add all those up, your total "cost of goods" per candle is

$14.30. If you sell the candle at the RRP of $30 plus tax, that means your profit (that's the cash you get to keep!) will look like this:

- Sale of the candle $33 (includes 10% tax)
- Less $14.30 cost of goods
- Equals $18.70 profit (which includes the 10% tax)

When you look at the above, what that sale did was (1) recoup the wholesale cost of the candle and (2) gave you nearly $19 in profit to keep. This means the money you can make is greater than the money you needed to invest ($18.70 profit is greater than $14.30 cost)

If you sold all six candles (which cost you $85.80 in total), you would have "grossed" (the total money you collected in selling all of them) a whopping $198 including tax.

When we subtract the total cost of goods from those total sales you're left with $112.20 in profit.

In sum, that's a really good retail product to sell!

But what if the RRP for the soy candle was only $20 plus tax. Would it be worth the outlay of $14.30 per candle to make $7.70 profit per one?

Maybe, if you're happy with that amount of profit. In this scenario, your profit is *less* than the cost of goods, so you have to sell twice as many in order to try and get close to the profit in the above scenario.

Of course, there are other variables that I haven't touched on in my soy candle example – such as product demand and import duty and taxes (if applicable) – so you do need to take some time to understand whether or not selling products is right for you.

Basic Profit Margin Calculator

To help, I've created a helpful Profit Margin Calculator Guide to help you work out if a product is potentially a good one to make profit from.

Just remember though, this is just a *guide* to help you. It's not going to guarantee profits or sales – so make sure you chat with your wholesaler about RRP, and if they don't have any, a chat with your accountant to get clarity around what sort of profits you need to make on retail sales for your specific business.

You can download my basic Profit Margin Calculator if you need a hand working out the profit margin on the products you want to sell: https://bit.ly/2BSwje7

Payment collection

The type of business you're going to open will probably dictate what sort of payment options you'll offer clients.

If your business is more a hobby or "side thing" – you might only want to accept cash, cheques, or direct bank deposits to keep things simple. But if you want a larger clientele, and more revenue, you need to do your best to open up the different ways people can pay you for your service and products. I've listed out the possible ways you can collect payment from clients.

- Cash
- Cheque
- Bank deposit / transfer
- Paypal
- Stripe
- Amazon Payments
- Traditional credit card machines (which are supplied by your bank)

The Setting Up Checklist

Once again, to make this process much easier, I've turned these items into a checklist (PDF) that you can download and work from: https://bit.ly/2TAsVzd

Chapter Recap

- The setting up checklist allows you to cover a lot of ground when preparing to set up your business.
- There's quite a lot of ground to cover when setting up a business, from fun things like decoration to serious stuff like pricing and payment collection.
- Every business will have different needs, and each state and country different requirements, so feel free to add more items to the checklist in the space provided.

Chapter 7: Marketing your business

Some people *love* marketing their business, while others would rather run the other way. The difference almost always comes back to the personality of the business owner.

Typically outgoing entrepreneurs have no problem setting off fireworks to wave down potential clients; whilst those who are more reserved and calculated tend to sit back and hope the client finds them.

Despite which personality type you resonate with – it's crucial you realise that your business *needs* good, solid marketing – whether you like it or not.

Marketing has a bit of a dark cloud over its head because there are some companies out there who mislead people in order to make sales. As such, a lot of people feel that taint by association – but please don't. True marketing is a benefit to everyone involved, and there's no need to be a pushy salesman or woman when utilising it.

How so? Well thankfully, because you have a passion for your natural therapy or healing business, creating the "good, solid marketing" I mentioned starts with you using 'Key 1 – Being genuine' as your foundations.

Boiling it all down, marketing is merely creating a genuine *connection* between (a) what you have to offer, and (b) those you know that offering will help.

That's it. No trickery required. When you make this brilliant connection with your audience, everything else flows like a springtime river.

But how exactly do you *make* that connection? Good question, and one I'm very happy to help you find the answer to!

1. Where's the connection?

Over the years, I've chatted with a lot of business owners who "get" that they need to do some sort of marketing, but there's a 'disconnect' in

what they end up doing.

In order to avoid wasting valuable time and money when building your business, you need to establish where the connection is between you and you clients.

In doing that, you need to get two things clear upfront:

1. What problem does my service or product solve?
2. Who is the person looking for my solution?

The first one's pretty easy to work out. For example, if you offer massages, you offer relaxation to resolve tension or provide relief to reduce pain. The problems were tension or pain, and your service solves them by providing relaxation or relief.

Now, let's try something not so easy. If you offer tarot card readings, you could say you offer some clarity to resolve confusion or provide possibilities to blocks. The problems were confusion and blockages, and your service solves them by providing clarity and possibilities.

Can you see the connection? *What you offer* is like a conduit – a channel say – that allows the solution to make its way to resolving your client's problem. Perhaps it won't be solved right away, maybe it's not for everybody – but the connection is genuine.

So before we move onto *who's* looking for your solution, let's write down what problems your service solves:

My service/s solves the problem of:

Now here's the harder part of the connection – *who* is looking for your service? Whenever I ask that of my coaching clients, they almost always say "everybody!" While I honour their enthusiasm, "everybody" is a *lot* of people – and it's near to impossible to connect with every single person on this planet. So we must narrow this down.

Don't' worry! I'm not going to get too technical here! I have no plans to make you write out a detailed client avatar or to analyse industry statistics. In saying that, if you want to – go for it – just don't get paralysed in the data.

In saying this, I do want you to consider a few things which I feel will help you get a better understanding of *who* is most likely to gravitate to your offering.

Now, do your best to *not* over-analyse when looking at the below elements of your ideal client:

- **Age** – you might think this is a no-brainer, but consider this. If you sell pre-school toys, you'd *think* the age of your market is under the age of five. But that's not actually true. The age of your ideal client is the parent, the person who can *buy the toy*. So it's probably older than you think!

- **Location** – this is particularly important if you have a physical location where people need to come see you or shop. Ask yourself, where does your ideal client spend most of their time? For example, if you offer horse agistment services, your clients are less likely to be hanging around the inner city.

- **Gender** – whilst we'll all open to serving genders equally, your service might be more appealing to one over the other. When I had the beauty salon with my mother, we always welcomed men (and have quite a few of them!), but our ideal clients were women – because they had no problems coming in on a regular basis to get services done.

- **Income level** – I don't necessarily want you to think, "$50,000 a year" when you see this component. But more so, if your service is $100 and requires re-booking every few weeks, then your ideal client probably needs to be someone who has a steady income. And of that income, some which is disposable.

- **Lifestyle** – this part of your ideal client's life is really important for you to understand. If you're a chiropractor, the chances are the lifestyle of your clients is less than desirable – they might sit all day which creates bad posture. And new meditation clients aren't usually already living a tranquil, serene existence (even though they can be!). But they're very likely to be busy professionals with lots of demands on their time – and just need some help getting a few moments of peace each week.

So now let's complete those elements of your ideal client, even if just loosely:

Age:	
Location:	
Gender:	
Income:	
Lifestyle:	

So now we're going to finalise the "who" your ideal client is by completing the sentence below! Just enter in what you wrote in the fields above in the appropriate sections below:

My ideal client is a _____ year old _____ and lives
(age) *(gender)*

in or around _____ earning _____
(location) *(income)*

living a very _____ type of life.
(lifestyle)

Now that we know what problem your service solves, and who the person is that needs it, establishing that genuine connection becomes so easy that the next steps fall into place!

2. Your tagline and USP

I briefly mentioned the term "tagline" in the brainstorming section of chapter 6, and I promised I'd give you a bit more about this so here we are.

To me, a tagline can serve one of two purposes: (1) it can summarise your business in just a few words, or (2) create some sort of drama or excitement. Or possibly both.

For the purposes of this book, as a new or existing business owner looking to grow, let's put the focus more on the first one: summarising your business in a few words.

This isn't to say you can't make your tagline compelling, but until you're at the level of Nike "*Just do it*" or McDonalds "*I'm lovin' it*" – those more emotive taglines won't do much to help you when you're starting out.

Let's use my business name, Natural Healer, as an example. Because the name is quite broad, to help potential customers, I have a tagline on my website that says next to the logo "*online training in energy & natural healing*". This says in just a handful of words, what it is that my business actually provides.

So unless your business name is "Core Fitness and Yoga" – you might want to consider adding a tagline that's helpful in clarifying *the what* that your business offers.

Take a moment to brainstorm a few ideas now – don't worry, no one's watching and you can always change your mind! Just start scribbling:

Tagline idea #1
Tagline idea #2
Tagline idea #3

The second component of this is for you to identify what your "unique selling proposition" (USP) is. What in the world is that? Simply put, it's how you'd sum up your business in a short sentence or two, including a mention of any special features of your service; something that not everybody else has and makes your business stand out from the rest.

For example, your Reiki sessions might always involve giving your clients a keepsake to remind them of the session so they can continue healing – perhaps a small crystal or affirmation card. As such, your USP could be *"We offer effective energy healing sessions anchored with a crystal memento at the end to help enhance your healing experience"*.

The USP doesn't have to be a physical token, it could revolve around experience of the practitioners or the inclusions of your service. Such as a yoga class which includes a one-minute Chakra cleansing exercise at the end.

To help establish what's unique about *your business* – and I know it will have something distinctive about it – take a moment to write down your unique selling proposition below:

USP idea #1
USP idea #2
USP idea #3

Once you get your USP nailed down, you should memorise it so if anyone ever asks what your business is about, you can explain it in 30-seconds or less with your USP.

3. The essentials

There are, what I consider, a few marketing "essentials" your business needs, no matter what size. Well, unless you're just running a hobby business with. Those essentials are:

1. **An online presence** – whether that's a website or a social media platform like Facebook, this gives prospective clients a place to learn more about you and possibly even book. Nowadays, if you *don't* have an online presence, you're not doing your business any favours.
2. **Brochure or business card** – depending on how many services you're going to offer will depend on whether you feel like you need one or both of these physical items. If you have a lot of services to select from, then a brochure is definitely a good idea. But if you offer only one or two services (that can be summed up quickly or apparent in your tagline) then a business card might suffice for now.
3. **A way for clients to book online** – having an online appointment program is a great way to allow clients the leisure of booking their own appointments (from within the parameters you set). I use Setmore[7] appointment scheduling (Simply Book Me[8] is also great) as they offer a great free package for new business, mobile app, and can be easily integrated within your website or even social platform.
4. **Packaged offer or incentive** – by having your services "bundled" at a slightly better price than what they'd cost independently, potential customers may spend a bit more with you up front in order to save that little bit in the long run. Or perhaps offer some sort of 'incentive' for your clients to refer you to others, or a 'get 10% after 5 massages' loyalty card, which encourages others to spread the word about how amazing you are!

---
[7] Find out more at Setmore https://www.setmore.com/?ref=melissacrowhurst
[8] To find out more, head to Simply Book Me https://simplybook.me/?ref=ida_2616

4. Free marketing

Unless it's your family or friends (who will naturally want to help you) the general public get *no upside* (that's benefit) from telling other people about your business.

So word of mouth, sharing blogs or posts on social media, and referrals are harder to come by – unless you have left a great impression upon them, or impacted someone in such a good way – that it compels them to let others know.

How do you do that? Remember my Five Keys to the Kingdom at the start of this book? And the genuine connection we spoke about earlier in this chapter? Well, if you can honestly do those – people will spread the word about your business – and at no charge.

Local paper or newsletter

If you're the type of business that enjoys getting involved and helping your community or local charities, be that through donations or volunteer work, there's an opportunity for your kindness to be rewarded. Even if it the good deeds you do has nothing to do with your business!

Most local papers or business newsletters are looking for good articles for their readers. As such, it's a good idea to reach out to their editorial department to see if they'd be keen on highlighting the good work you're doing for the community.

When they cover your story, chances are they will happily mention your business, or take a photo of you in your logo shirt, in the article, too! This a win-win-win for everybody involved! A win for the community, a win for the paper, and a win for your business

Social media

If you have a social media page like Facebook or Instagram, it's *obviously* an easy, fast and free way for you to promote yourself. However, just keep in mind that these platforms are actually about *community* and sharing – not overt advertising.

So whilst it's a great idea to post a grand opening special, or a sale, make sure you don't constantly fill people's newsfeeds with self-promotion and sales ads. You probably know yourself, if you continuously feel like you're being "sold to" and not getting any value from a page you're following – you'll just stop noticing their posts, or unfollow them altogether.

Remember, your social followers want *helpful, informative* content from you – not a sales pitch. At least not all the time. People realise you're a business, so posting a special or update about your business won't alarm them, just not every day, all day.

When you're about to hit "publish", just keep in mind *why* you started your business to begin with – to help others. That way, when you share, it's with others' best interests in mind, increasing the chances of people further sharing your information. Why? Because it's genuine.

Organic search engine optimization

I'll just briefly touch on what's called organic "search engine optimization" (SEO) – a free form of online marketing that's connected to how visible your online presence (like a website, socials, or some other platform like an Etsy store) is when someone types a term in the search box of a web browser.

But first, let's translate that technical internet-speak to English!

When used in conjunction with SEO, the term "organic" means you didn't have to pay an advertiser to help you attract visitors to your website.

A "search engine" is a platform like Google, Yahoo, or Bing – which enables people to search for things. Whilst "optimization" (in this context) is all about ensuring your online presence includes the terms and content that your ideal customer is looking for.

The term "rankings" is associated with *where* on the search results page you appeared when someone typed in that term.

So if you have a website, you want to ensure that you include terms and content on each page, which gives a potential client the answer/s to what they were originally searching for.

For example, if you offer a numerology service on your website – think the following when finding the term you want to make predominant on that page: *"What would my ideal client be typing in the search engines to find my service?"*

They're probably not typing "What is numerology", right? They're probably typing "numerology reading" or perhaps "numerologist in Atlanta".

From there, you'll want to include content (text, images, video) which then give your potential client all the answers they may have about your numerology service, and then the option to book or buy.

I highly recommend, if you have a website, that you educate yourself[9] more on what SEO is and how you help your website rank "organically" – so free.

5. Paid marketing

This is the most common way businesses get attention, partly because it's easier (you just have to pay for exposure) and partly because it's the quickest way to reach an audience who know nothing about you.

There are *a lot of ways* you can pay for marketing – and trust me – marketing agencies and advertising companies will take your money irrespective of whether they think you'll do well out of it or not.

---

[9] This site is a great resource for SEO education: https://bit.ly/1zMwfYS

So if you're going to pay for marketing (advertising), then it's worth doing a little bit of research beforehand!

Thankfully, you've already done a heap of ground work up to this point (so that's a hint! If you haven't completed the exercises in this chapter – stop – and go do them now!) so this next bit of research won't be daunting.

Google Ads

If you don't know what Google Ads is, then I recommend you watch this short video from them which summarises is quite nicely: https://youtu.be/cOTMWqwUXPU

The Google Ads platform can be quite overwhelming in and of itself, let alone understanding all the intricacies behind tracking, cost per click (CPC), conversion rates and so on.

But in saying that, since Ads is part of Google, you are practically guaranteed a spot somewhere on the first page if you're willing to pay for it. Before you dive into paid advertising like this though, you just want to make sure you understand a bit about organic SEO (mentioned in the section before this) and ensure the website page you send your potential client to has a few essentials on it:

- A clear explanation of the problem your service or product solves.
- The price, or benefit.
- The service inclusions, or what they'll get.
- Who you are and why you're awesome (note: if a prospective client has never heard of you, this information can be the reason they finally decide to buy!)
- An "add to cart" or booking or subscribe button – or some other form which collects the information from your new visitor.

Google Ads can be rewarding, but unless you have a bit of a marketing budget available, and have the time to learn and nurture your campaign, you may prefer to try another option to get your "feet wet" in the world of paid marketing, so to speak.

Social media

Now this is the *other side of the coin* to social media than what I discussed in the free marketing section. Most social platforms have an avenue where you can *pay* to promote your business.

Just like with Google Ads, the platforms can be tricky to operate, so make sure you do a bit of research on how to best use your preferred platform. Also, ensure you have included the essentials (listed in the section before) for wherever you're sending that potential client to.

Social media marketing can be incredibly targeted (age, sex, income, interests, habits, etc.) but unless you keep a close eye on the campaign, all your budget can get used up very quickly, or you could end up exceeding what you wanted to spend.

Remember, if you're going to pay for each time someone "clicks" your ad – you want to make sure you're doing it right for the best possible results! As such, I highly suggest you use Facebook's online learning centre[10] to get educated on how to advertise on it, Instagram, Messenger, and Whatsapp.

Old school paper

Even in our digital age, my real mailbox still gets stuffed with catalogues and papers every day.

So while it's maybe not the most progressive form of marketing, it could be effective if your target market isn't one that uses the internet all the time.

---

[10] The Facebook learning centre is free: https://bit.ly/2zo28Kp

For example, if you offer services to the elderly, or people who tend to be out working the land all day, internet surfing and social searching might not be high on their daily routine. But checking the letterbox probably is!

The more expensive paper option is to take out an advertisement, which can be very costly. As such, you'll want to make sure your ad has a good "call to action" for the reader – such as a limited grand opening special price, or "bring this coupon in for a free 15 minute session".

Alternatively, you can print up flyers or brochures and pop them into mailboxes (as long as it's legal for you to do so), or hang them in a community hall or local shops.

If you go this option, I highly recommend you use recycled paper, let's be kind to our mother earth. ☺

6. Two effective strategies

I know there's a lot of information to take in when it comes to marketing, let alone business! So I won't throw you in the deep in here! Below you'll find, what I consider, a great marketing plan for any business. Of course, you'll need to chop and change it to suit your needs, as some things may not work for your business, and I won't know your own special strategies!

But I've provided them here as a *guide*, to help your chances of improving that *connection* we spoke about at the start of this chapter!

For new or small business

I touched on this technique a bit earlier in the book, but so you have it in one spot, here is a wonderful little marketing strategy for a new business:

1. Offer your services for free – asking for a testimonial in return; and,

2. Book yourself solid (or as much as you can handle) with your free sessions; and,
3. Over-deliver during the session so you impress your client; and,
4. Once you're done, ask them to go ahead and book their next session, at a slightly discounted rate.
5. Then after that – they'll be hooked on you and willing to pay your full price!

As you do that strategy, start compiling a list of your client's contact details, so you can market to them directly if and when you need to.

For example, if you're schedule is looking empty one week, you can reach out to existing clients easily with a special offer specifically for that slow week in order to fill it up. It's better to have more bookings at a slight discount than none at all!

For existing or larger businesses

Once you've built up your business a bit more, I recommend the following in order to help you work out what's necessary to establish the recurring income your business needs to thrive.

Most businesses need repeat clients to maintain its stability, so you need to work out what your "retention rate" is – that's how many people end up becoming a regular client.

1. **Retention Rate** - Work out, for every five customers, how many of them become a 'repeat' (aka. regular) customer.

For example, if for every five clients you see, three of them become 'repeat' clients – that's a 60% retention rate (3 divided by 5 = 0.60)

If your retention rate is bad (say you only retain one in every five) – then you need to ask yourself *"Why is that? What's wrong with my system or service that's keeping people from re-booking and coming back?"*

Once you work out your "retention rate" it's now time to work out how often clients come back to see you, giving you an idea of expected income per regular client over a longer period of time.

2. **Frequency** – Work out if regular clients see you once a month, once a quarter, once a year?

Now that you know your retention rate and your client frequency, it's time to work out the average spend per client visit.

3. **Average Spend** – How much does a regular client typically spend with you, per session?

Combining the knowledge you now have with client retention, frequency and average spend will ultimately give you the parameters of your marketing budget, which I'll explain now.

Let's just say, for every five customers, you "retain" three as regulars – that's a 60% retention rate. A regular client will come every month to see you. And the average spend for each visit is $50.

- 5 clients = 3 retained as regular (the other two may never come back)
- 1 customer session = $50
- x 12 months = $600

This means for every 5 clients see you, there's potential to earn $1,800+ per year, on a regular basis.

To dive in deeper, if you divide the $1,800 by the five clients in total, then every single person who walks in the door is worth up to $360 each to you (that's $1,800 divided by 5 = $360).

Knowing this figure gives you a bit of a heads-up on how much you can spend to acquire a new client.

How so? If for every person who comes to see you is worth $360, on average, over the course of a year, then ask yourself – how much are you willing to spend to get that person in the door?

Would it be reasonable to spend, say, $100 in advertising spend to get that one new client? The short answer is yes ☺

So in this example, your marketing budget to acquire one new client is $100. Granted, you can spend more or less – it's ultimately up to you. But this at least gives you some parameters on what you can spend in advertising. And you also need to ensure you can *retain* those clients that come see you – because you've spent $100 to acquire each one.

So how would you go about getting these clients?

You *lower the hurdle* to get them in the door. What I mean by this is you can do something like a special once-off low-offer; instead of $50 a session, it's $25 to see you for the first time.

Why would you do this? Because, based on what we've just worked out, you *know* that for every 5 clients, you'll end up with 3 regulars who will be worth $1,800 over the year.

So taking a bit of a "hit" on the first session is just your way of getting them to try your amazing services, as you will over-deliver, and they will re-book – creating the recurring income your business needs.

So here's your strategy:

1. Work out your retention rate
2. Work out your regular client frequency
3. Work out your regular client's average spend
4. From that, work out what you'll be willing to spend to acquire one new client (aka. your marketing budget)
5. Work out your special "offer" or "promotion" that you'll use to advertise to get those potential clients
6. Do an amazing job, rinse and repeat!

Marketing Budget Calculator

To help with these numbers, I've created a Marketing Budget Calculator Guide. But as mentioned before, this is just a *guide* to help you. You can download it here: https://bit.ly/2CfBjK4

7. Ongoing marketing

One of the biggest mistakes I see new business make is that they'll spend a bit of time and marketing up front – but after their grand opening or launch – they sit back on their laurels.

It's a big world out there, with a lot of people doing the best they can to be found and to be heard. So even if you opened your business with a bang, it doesn't mean *everybody* in your reach knows about you.

Business is not "set and forget" – remember, you are the captain of this ship. So you must pay attention, assess, and adjust your plan as unexpected waves, tides, and winds try to throw you off course.

So if you want to ensure you keep up the excitement and momentum you had when you first opened your business – do *not* forget to keep your marketing going - ongoing.

Whether it's at a small budget, or just done during quieter periods, you need to *help your business help you*. Then over time, as your business grows, your marketing budget can grow as well – to ensure you continue to reach and help more people with your service.

Perhaps you'll offer a once-a-month special, or do a little contest, or announce a new service – whatever it is, put some marketing fuel (be it dollars or just elbow grease) into it each time.

Chapter Recap

- In order for marketing to be effective, you have to know what problem your service or product solves, and who's looking for your solution.
- A tagline quickly helps someone identify with your business name or brand.
- A "Unique Selling Proposition" (USP) is what makes your business different to others.
- There are free and paid marketing options, which you should get some basic education in before you go deeper.
- Some level of marketing for your business should continue – ongoing - even if you're doing well.

Chapter 8: Running your business

You've made it! You've done all the training, pre-planning, preparation, set up, marketing and here you are – running your very own business. To say I'm proud of you is an understatement! Everyone can dream, but not many can take the necessary steps to turn it into a reality, so let's take a moment to celebrate!

GO YOU!

With everything under your belt, as I mentioned at the end of the last chapter – it's now time to ensure you stay *on* course, not just with your business goals, but to that inner moral compass of yours.

Let's take a moment to remember Keys 3 and 4 – Being responsive and Being understanding. Flip back to those early sections if you can't remember them, because they will give you the *grace* and *patience* you need to operate your business in a way that keeps most situations in "check" and the stress to a minimum.

While everybody is going to have a different type of business, I'm going to do my best to list out some operational gold for you to follow!

Create processes

Having some basic processes documented is a very good idea – especially for things that happen repeatedly. This isn't just a great way to prepare for growth, but also sets some parameters around expectations – be that between you and your partners, clients, or employees.

So even if you're a one-person show right now, don't discount putting pen-to-paper to document things you might want to get off your plate in future.

For example, if you have a certain way you like to answer the phone or greet clients – wouldn't it be handy to have something ready to help you with training the day that you hire a receptionist?

Or perhaps after you complete a massage, you always pour a cup of warm tea then show the client to a relaxation spot to 'come back to reality'. If you hired another massage therapist – would it give you peace of mind to know they've learned your process so all your clients get your star treatment?

Creating processes is *not* a difficult feat. It's simply opening up a notebook, or word document, and writing out:

1. What the process is, as the title (e.g. How to greet clients)

2. Then explain Step 1, Step 2, Step 3 and so on (eg. Step 1. When someone walks in, always make eye contact and smile. Step 2. Ask them how you can help, Step 3....)
3. Saving them somewhere handy – if a physical piece of paper, perhaps you can start a store manual folder you keep at the front desk; if a digital document save it into a folder and name it accordingly so you can find it fast.

Having your core processes documented isn't just a great way for you to maintain customer service and service delivery consistency, but can also *add value* to your business as it grows.

Manage your schedule

It goes without saying that you will most likely use a booking tool of some sort, even if it's a physical appointment book to start with.

If you don't already have a reliable booking platform that can handle multiple services, multiple staff, and multiple calendars – and that's easy to use – I recommend that you sign up to Setmore or Simply Book Me.

As I mentioned in the marketing chapter, Setmore is the program I use for my client bookings (and Simply Book Me is great too). They even have a free option, find out more check the links in the resources section at the end of this book.

If you don't use a booking program to schedule and remind you of appointments, then I *highly recommend* you put a solid process in place that will remind you when client bookings are.

One good way to do this is to have a physical appointment book, and if you aren't doing this work full-time, to set reminders in your phone for when your bookings are.

A word of warning though! I don't recommend you manage bookings solely via your phone calendar – it will only take the device failing or getting lost for everything to be lost forever. And you won't have any backup!

Conducting a session

Irrespective of whether you call your service type an appointment, session, booking, class, or something else – you should have some basic steps in place so your clients are assured of your consistency as a professional. Here's an example of how a session might be conducted:

1. Greet client with eye contact and a smile as they arrive
2. If applicable, allow them to sit and complete your intake form (more on that shortly), and check back in with them in a few minutes.
3. Make 'small talk' with them as you lead them to the spot where you'll be conducting the session. Simple things like "How's your day been?" or "Wow, how cool is the weather today!" This just keeps awkward silence from developing in those short moments before the session.
4. If it's their first time with you, explain some of the things you need them to do, or what they may expect during the session.
5. Conduct your session.
6. Once done, allow your client some appropriate time and space to 'come back' to the real world. This might just be a few minutes.
7. If you have time, it's a good idea to once again – make some small talk, but specifically about the session: "How do you feel now?" or "Did you have any questions?"
8. If appropriate, ask the client if they'd like to re-book with you in a certain amount of time. If the decline, be gracious and say something like, "That's okay! You know how to get in touch if you ever need me again" and ensure they have your brochure or business card. Some more shy business owners might feel uncomfortable doing this, but I just want to remind that asking

right after a good session is a great way to keep your schedule full!
9. Ensure you 'send-off' your client with the same eye contact and smile
10. Take a breather and relax ☺

Client intake form

Client intake forms are a really important part of any service-based business. Whether it's meditation and yoga, chiropractic or massage, or energy healing and Reiki – gathering up some client history can really help you understand how to best help.

Furthermore, you have the opportunity to ask clients for their contact details on an intake form, and to specify there if they're happy to receive marketing material from you from time to time.

You might only need to obtain very basic info, or perhaps quite a lot – it will come down to your industry's best practice. I suggest you contact your training provider as they're likely to have a template for you to use.

Alternatively, here's the client intake form I provide to my Reiki and energy healing students, so you have an example: https://bit.ly/2SgjuQe

Post session follow-up

This step might not be necessary depending on the type of service you provide, but I think it's good practice.

And to be clear, a post-session follow-up is *not* a 'marketing' email or call. Although it could be loosely considered a small part of marketing in that it strengthens the connection you have with your client with good customer service.

I suggest you contact your client about a week or so after your session. Whether it's via email or phone call, it's a great way to find out a few things:

- How they're feeling since they last saw you; and/or,
- If you can offer any tips or suggestions to continue to improve; and/or,
- If they had any feedback or a testimonial for you (if they didn't provide it while they were with you).

Because there is no "sales" pressure in your follow-up call, you'll likely get honest feedback and a genuinely good feeling knowing your client has done well since they last saw you.

To make life even easier, many leading booking platforms (like the ones I've already mentioned) have email follow-ups as part of their system so this can just automatically happen after your client's appointment. That means this brilliant level of customer service happens without you needing to remember to do it!

Responses and reviews

None of us will have an issue reading and responding to glowing reviews for our business! As such, I recommend you still always thank those people who take the time to respond to your follow-up process, or to anyone who leaves a review for you.

But what about the negative reviews?

Remember Keys 3 and 4 – ' Being Understanding' and 'Being Responsive'? That when those two keys kick in. Whether or not you knew the experience was 'less than stellar' for that client at the time, it's impossible to make everybody happy, all the time.

Everyone experiences life in different ways, and some people use negative feedback towards others as a method of venting some other issues they have deep inside.

What's most important here is that you *be understanding* of this difference. You would've done your best at the time, and if that didn't register with your client, there's not much you can do now to make them see otherwise.

So with your *understanding* 'cap' on, *still* respond to that client. But in the kindest way you can – even if it's just a few words like, "Thank you, I appreciate the time you took to let me know this."

Depending on the situation and the client's personality, you might go as far as apologising and advising you're happy to offer a discount, or some sort of incentive, if they'd like to give your business another shot.

For some situations and clients, it's best to just say "Thanks" and let it go. For others, you might want to really try to win that client back.

The decision to let go, or to win back, will ultimately fall with you. But to keep your business's reputation in good stead – *always respond* (even if it's a public review) and *always* do it in a way that shows your level of professionalism and understanding.

Operating expenses

Remember when I touched on "capital purchases" and "cost of goods" earlier in the book? Well, generally speaking, operating expenses are pretty much everything else!

To be a bit more clear, operating expenses are the costs which are indirectly related to you being able to provide a product or service. So these things *aren't* the goods or service themselves, and they *aren't* capital purchases (assets), but they play an important part in facilitating making everything run.

I want to mention this only because a lot new business owners tend forget about the vast array of expenses they will inevitably incur just to operate a business.

I'll list out some of the more common operational expenses below, and suggest you use some sort of accounting software to keep track of them (if your accountant isn't doing that for you):

- Liability insurance to cover mishaps that may happen in or at your business
- Insurance to cover damage to any other assets like your stock, building, or vehicle
- Professional association memberships
- Mortgage or rent
- Utilities, such as electricity, gas, and water
- Other outgoings such as property tax, local council or city taxes, special taxes for advertising or for permits
- Telephone, mobile phone, and internet connection
- Subscriptions to programs and software
- Bank fees and interest
- Marketing and advertising costs
- Other sundries, like tea room or staff kitchen supplies

Wages and related expenses

Now with capital purchases, cost of goods/service, and operational expenses all under your belt – here's the last one: wages! This cost is usually separated from the other expenses of your business because they're usually regulated and have obligatory conditions.

For example, as an employer, you're responsible to pay whatever the applicable income tax is, to your taxation office, at the appropriate time each quarter or year. You may also have obligations to make payments towards retirement funds or healthcare.

This means you need to consider these obligations carefully and ensure you have that money tucked away so when it's time to pay – you can. Remember, these are expenses are directly related – and can impact – the livelihoods of others, so please take them seriously!

One last note, having independent contractors or sub-contractors working for you is *different* to having employees. So please (yes, you guessed it!) speak with your accountant if you need further guidance.

Managing staff well

Nobody likes a pushy or controlling manager – nobody. But at the same time, not many people like a wishy-washy or indecisive one either! So how do you manage staff, and how do you do it well?

For me, the key to effectively managing staff is about balancing yourself on the fine line of being understanding while holding *others* responsible for their duties. That, and to *not* be bothered if someone *doesn't* think *"you're the best boss ever!"*

During the hay-day of the retail enterprise my husband and I ran, we had over 20 employees on the roster, as well as contractors who did regional sales for us. No matter how fun I tried to make things, or considerate I tried to be to everyone's needs – I can promise you, there were those who didn't like me. They were never rude or mean, they just didn't like me.

I'm not trying to say people aren't going to like you if you manage them. What I'm trying to point out is that, as a business owner (and likely manager of people), it's imperative you keep your "need" to be liked in check.

As a manager of others, you are essentially being the good steward of that ship (aka. business) of yours – and everyone has a role to play to keep that thing afloat.

There is a component of needing 'thicker' skin for the role of manager, and it goes without saying that not everybody is well suited for that job. But if you're in the situation of *having* to be the manager, and business owner, just do your best.

Just keep those Keys to the Kingdom (that I taught you at the start of the book) in mind if you're the only person who can fill those managerial shoes.

Being fair, kind and considerate whilst honouring your staff's skills by letting them do their jobs – all while holding them accountable for their actions – will allow you to be a very good manager. And if an employee ends up honestly liking you as a person as well as their manager, then that's a bonus!

Self-care and rest

Entrepreneurs and business owners are usually very guilty when it comes to *not* doing sufficient self-care and rest. And that's probably because you want to fill every possible moment with forward motion – there's a mixture of excitement for your growing business, shouldering responsibility for others, and caring about the quality of product or service you provide to your clients – thus wider community.

In the early days of my many businesses, I struggled to rest and take true care of myself. I often found myself doing *"just one more email"*, or taking on one more client, or staying up late organising a storage room, or something else. Then, I'd end up so exhausted the next day that I'd get a cold or have so little motivation that I was completely useless – or both!

What did I learn? That at the end of the day sweet friend, if you are unwell and unrested – so is your business.

There are many times, still to this day, where I *could* just keep on working, keep on helping, keep on replying to my many students. And while it's sometimes hard to say no – you need to.

I have come to understand that if I don't honour my physical self (aka. my spiritual house) as much as I do my sacred self (aka. my spirit itself) – there will be no one to captain my ship. Who will take care of all those beautiful people I help if I cannot be *fully present*?

As such, I have a *minimum down-time* routine that works well for me: I *always* meditate each day (even if for just few minutes), do yoga, and get a good night's rest (a full 7 – 8 hours).

I will work my little heart out in all my other waking hours – but those moments of rest time are mine. No one else's.

Just a side note, doing something like yoga or meditation doesn't have to take hours either. In particular meditation[11] can be done sporadically throughout your day and within minutes – and no need for specific clothes or tools.

I strongly suggest, like I do for myself, that you work out some sort of rest (aka. 'me time'), too. Otherwise you may find yourself financially successful one day, but not in a healthy mindset or body to enjoy the fruits of your labour.

Remember, if you take care of yourself first, *then* you're in a good place to help and take care of others. As your wonderful business grows, your processes improve, and your team takes on more responsibility – you'll find you can have longer weekends, or annual holidays. And you'll take them well deserved.

Chapter Recap

- One of the most important things you can do early on in order to manage your business well is to set up processes.
- Being a good steward of your business involves managing people in a kind and fair way whilst holding them accountable for their actions.
- Doing regular self-care is vital for the long term success of a business. If you're unwell and unrested – so is your business.

---

[11] I even teach how to meditate quickly in my online course here:
https://naturalhealer.com.au/product/learn-to-meditate-course/

Chapter 9: Growing with your business

By the time you get to this point in your journey, you're a seasoned business owner. You've opened your doors, you've worked with clients, you've experienced a huge array of challenges and triumphs – and look at you! You've come out the other side! Funnily enough, you soon realise that the "other side" is just a bigger, bolder ocean to sail!

So you can easily tread water by continuing to do what you've always done. There's nothing wrong with that at all if you're happy as you are.

But if you're not fully content with where your business is at, or have bigger dreams that add a sparkle to your eyes, then it's time to grow your business more. How do you do that? It's time to re-assess, plan, and set your compass for the new journey!

Where are you at now?

Because economic climates can change like the weather, before considering growth, get some data under your belt and then have a good chat with your accountant.

I believe the best way to get true data is to actually operate as a business for at least two years. This gives you the ability to compare how things are tracking from the first to second year, as well as catch if your business has any seasonal fluctuations.

Using your actual business's historical data allows you to more accurately forecast into the future. And one of the best ways to do this is by getting your annual Profit & Loss (P&L) statements from your accountant.

If you're part-way through another year of trading, also try and get your book keeping up to date so you can get an estimated P&L (based on averages) for the current year.

Getting this information not only allows you to see how your business has grown over the previous years, but if it's on track with that ultimate goal of yours!

Where do you want to be ultimately?

Remember back when we did the initial planning (back in Chapter 5), the last few items were about getting clarity on your financial goal, your work-life goal, and your ultimate goal.

If you review those now – how are you tracking in each?

Are you knocking it out of the park, or do you need to do some more work to achieve them?

Let's quickly re-assess those goals now:

Initial financial goal	Current finances	Difference
_____	_____	_____
example: $1,000 per week	example: $650 per week	example: -$350 per week
Initial work-life goal	**Actual situation**	**Difference**
_____	_____	_____
example: 35 hour per week	example: 50 hours per week	example: -25 hours per week
Initial ultimate goal	**Same?**	**Difference**
_____	_____	_____
example: go global/franchise	example: yes	example: none

If you're in the negative with the financial and work-balance goals, then before you can grow and expand – you need to hit these first. Or at least see incremental and continuous improvement towards them.

This is important because as the business owner, if you don't have some sense of accomplishment and fulfilment along your journey with these goals – even if you're super positive – subconscious resentment and real physical exhaustion can wear you down.

How can you truly get excited about raising your sails for the next journey if you're not seeing progression in the original one? It might be an exciting thought, but don't spread yourself too thin – in particular if it puts you at extreme risk in finances or health.

Is it time to grow and expand?

If you've stayed true to the course of your journey (including getting lost, getting back on track, going slow and going fast!) and are moving towards the goals we just went over – then once you see steady advancement or you hit them – then it's time to raise those sails!

But if it's not the right time to proactively grow and expand – don't be disheartened! Everyone experiences life in their own way, at their own pace – and that's the same for business! Stay true to the course and the growth will come!

Preparing to grow!

There are so many possibilities with growth and expansion, so let's jot down your ideas now to start getting a feel for what you need to do, and how much it's going to cost:

What is your growth or expansion idea? Do want to hire staff so you can take on more clients? Is it time to open a second location, launch a retail store or finally franchise your business to others?

_____

_____

How much more in revenue do you expect your business to receive as a result of this idea?

_____

_____

Up-front costs

Do you need to purchase more products or get a bigger (or another) location?

_____

What are these costs?

_____

_____

Will you need to increase your marketing budget once it's done?

_____

What are these costs?

_____

Do you need to hire more staff?

_____

What are these costs?

_____

What other once-off costs are there? (legal documents for franchising? Trademarking?)

_____

_____

Tally up all your upfront costs:

Other costs

How much will this increase your operational costs?

_____

Are there any other one-off costs you'll incur?

_____

_____

How much extra money will you need to help "buffer" any fluctuations in cash flow in the first three months after your plan has taken action?

_____

_____

Tally up all your other costs:

Finances

How much cash in the bank do you have for this growth?

_____

_____

Do you need to borrow money to implement your plan? What are the fees, interest rates, and repayments?

_____

_____

Now you've got these ideas sketched out, populate the basic figures below to get a real snapshot of your growth or expansion plan. Once you've done that – yes, you guessed it – head back to your accountant to see if these are feasible for your financial situation before you set sail!

Your current revenue

_____

Increase in revenue from growth/expansion

_____

Upfront costs + once-off costs

_____

Cash in the bank

_____

Financing

_____

Financing repayment amount

_____

Term

_____

To make things even easier, I suggest you go back and use elements of the initial planning checklist to help you cover off on your growth and expansion plans!

How do I turn things around?

But what if right now 'growing with your business' has nothing to do with expansion, but more to do with keeping your head above water?

It's not uncommon to see businesses posting a small loss in the first year or two of business. A that's largely due to the set-up costs in addition to the learning curve around marketing, sales, and operations.

But even with the small losses, the actual costs to run your business should still be covered – and things should be looking positive going into the next year.

If that's not the case for you, and you're seeing big losses with no end in sight – then it's time to change strategy. Just remember – a faltering business isn't a failure – it's a sign. It only becomes a failure when you ignore the signs.

A lot of business owners ignore the signs, even unknowingly, because they're afraid that acknowledging them somehow means the idea was bad, the business was bad, and as such – that they're bad.

I'm here to tell you, if you're business takes a turn downward - **you are not a failure**. You took a chance that most people will never have the courage to do: start a business.

What might have started off as a good idea a few years ago may not be a good one now. Or perhaps new competitors have come onto the playing field, or the financial climate has changed, or maybe – just maybe – the service you offer isn't the right fit for the market right now.

As a side note, I'm a true believer in manifesting! So much so I even wrote a book[12] about it!

---

[12] Real Manifesting: Hacking the Law of Attraction:
https://naturalhealer.com.au/product/real-manifesting-law-of-attraction-book/

But even in that, I teach readers that setting goals, then continuously feeling, thinking, saying, and – very importantly – doing actions that move you closer to the finish line are all critical to success.

And that's the same with business. So look at your business for what it is, see its failings, and work out a game plan to right the wrongs.

Business health check

Go through and honestly answer the below questions to help give you some insight on *where* you may be going wrong with your business.

As you answer them, you might start to get ideas – write them down! Then start working out steps you can take to implement changes and new ideas.

1. Are you getting many enquiries or sales leads?

If yes, of those enquiries and leads, are most of them becoming paying clients?

_____

If no, ask yourself, Why? Is the product or service of good quality? Priced right? Is the problem it solves clearly displayed on the marketing? Where and how are you marketing the business?

_____

_____

2. With the sales you do make, are clients coming back for more or referring others?

If yes, that's great! But are you remembering to obtain their contact details so you can send them updates and offers directly via phone, email, or mail?

_____

If no, ask yourself, why? Are treating them with respect and making them feel special? Are you giving them reason to trust and refer others to you?

_____

_____

3. Are you making enough profit on each sale?

If yes, that's great! Are there other ways you can increase your profit margins, such as ordering in bulk?

Picking up instead paying for shipping? Suggesting small cost add-ons to your service which increase the overall sale amount?

_____

If no, remember the pricing section in Chapter 6? You want to ensure you make enough profit with each transaction in order to cover your operating expenses, wages, and get some profit, too!

Go back to your invoices and really crack down on how much your products or services are costing you – and see where you can increase the profit margin.

In addition to the profit margin tips above, perhaps you need to stop selling a particular item or offering a certain service (because it's losing you money), or re-negotiate the pricing with the supplier.

_____

_____

4. Are your expenses or wages in check?

If yes and you're running a pretty tight ship in terms of expenses, then chances are you need to look at questions #1, #2, and #3 more intensely.

___

If no, it's time to re-assess where there could be unnecessary or excessive spending in for your business. Are you purchasing extra supplies that aren't needed for some time? Are you taking staff out to lunch or dinner too much? Are you putting personal expenses through under your business?

Have you chatted with your accountant to get their perspective on your expense and wage bill?

___

___

5. Are you noticing more negative feedback than positive?

If yes, then it's time to re-assess who, what, and how you're delivering your service or product.

Perhaps the person on the 'front lines' isn't good with people? Or the product isn't on par with the client's quality expectations? Or perhaps there's a better way to conduct your service?

___

___

6. Do you still have the same desire to succeed as you did when you first started?

If yes, that's brilliant – so now go through your answers to really uncover where the 'holes' are in your ship – and start plugging them up!

_____

If no, then that's even *more* reason to go through all these question and answer them honestly – and with most intensity.

Then go back to your original goal, then go *within yourself* and ask: Why did you start this business? Do you have something good to offer this world? Remind yourself that these are all signposts pointing you in the *right* direction now!

_____

_____

If it hasn't become obvious by now (by the sheer number of mentions in the book) your accountant is integral in helping you steer and grow your business!

So once you've completed this check list, and you decide change strategy, get your accountant's help to crunch the numbers for your new game plan!

Chapter Recap

- Understanding where you are now, compared to where you want to be, is a great way to see if you're ready for proactive growth and expansion.
- Just like everything else in business, you should plan your growth or expansion strategy to ensure you don't put yourself in a compromising position in future.
- If you need to turn things around in your business, following the business health checklist will shine a light on areas that need fixing and possibly inspire you!

Chapter 10: You've got this!

As we come to a close, just remember that a thriving business is *at the service* of the public, it provides something of need to others, and can be a valuable contributor to the community – if not the greater good of this world.

As such, being at the helm of a successful business that helps others is a noble position – and I honour you for starting and growing one!

Giving back

As your business becomes self-sufficient, in that it covers its expenses and posts profits, as an *Infinitely Gracious Business Owner* you may want to consider how you can *give back* to the community which helped you thrive.

I personally find this is an integral part of business growth and success. How? In every aspect of life (including business) there's a continual and infinite circuit of rebirth: potential, growth, expand, decline – then repeat.

Allowing the positive energy (which helped your business prosper) continue moving forward – instead of holding onto it – means you *shared* that good energy with others, which is rewarding in and of itself.

Then as a result of that, you freed up the necessary space within to be able *accept more* into your life.

So, how do you do *give back*? It's easy! Your business can simply give charitable donations, or sponsor worthwhile events or causes, or provide free services or products for fundraisers. Go with whatever feels right to you, when it's time.

Once again, chat with your accountant about whether it's a good time for you to start giving back, and how you can do it within your business.

Thank you

While business is both exhilarating and rewarding, it can be tiring and challenging, too!

But if you keep the keys to the kingdom I taught you firmly attached to your belt, all your planning in hand, and love in your heart – your business success is just across that threshold!

I cannot begin to *thank you enough* for allowing me to be a part of creating and growing your very own business!

All the words written on these pages came right from my heart, inspired by what I myself do in my own business, so I do truly hope you've found my experiences as valuable as I do!

Thank you for your time, for trusting me, and for being an amazing soul who wants to share their beautiful gifts and talents with the rest of the world!

Infinitely Gracious Business Owner certification

If you feel you've been able to weave the skills from these pages into your business journey, I trust that you will *never* stray away from that inner moral compass of yours!

As such, you should be really proud of yourself – because I'm proud of you! So, if you'd like to become certified as one of my *Infinitely Gracious Business Owner*s, then all you need to do is enrol an complete the course that complements this book and pass a short final review for certification:

https://naturalhealer.com.au/product/natural-therapy-reiki-business-course

Keep shining that bright light within you – the world needs what you have to give! **#biglove**

Chapter 11: Helpful Resources

I've referenced quite a lot of helpful resources throughout the book, so to make it easier for you to refer to in future, I'll list them all – and more – here!

Note, some of the website URLs are quite long, so I've used the URL shortener "Bitly" to make some of them more manageable. I did that just for ease for typing, once you enter it, it will redirect to the correct business URL.

Books

- Melissa's *Real Manifesting: Hacking the Law of Attraction* book https://naturalhealer.com.au/product/real-manifesting-law-of-attraction-book/ (if you're in the USA you might want to purchase off Amazon postage: https://amzn.to/2C8HK1j)
- *Money Master the Game: 7 Simple Steps to Financial* Freedom - Tony Robbins https://amzn.to/2TJFCYU

- *Awaken the Giant Within : How to Take Immediate Control of Your Mental, Emotional, Physical and Financial Destiny!* - Tony Robbins https://amzn.to/2CvEaPd
- *Think and Grow Rich: The Original, an Official Publication* - Napoleon Hill https://amzn.to/2TBDr9w
- *Ultimate Guide to Google AdWords: How to Access 100 Million People in 10 Minutes (Ultimate Series)* - Perry Marshall https://amzn.to/2UE1uRx
- *Ultimate Guide to Facebook Advertising: How to Access 1 Billion Potential Customers in 10 Minutes (Ultimate Series)* - Perry Marshall https://amzn.to/2FcnL3H
- *Instagram Secrets: The Underground Playbook for Growing Your Following Fast, Driving Massive Traffic & Generating Predictable Profits* - Jeremy McGilvrey https://amzn.to/2FcM6Gz

Certificate courses and training

- The *Infinitely Gracious Business Owner* Certification Course https://naturalhealer.com.au/product/natural-therapy-reiki-business-course
- All of Melissa's other online courses https://naturalhealer.com.au/product-category/online-courses/
- Discover Massage Australia (tell them I sent you so they look after you!) https://www.discovermassage.com.au/
- First Aid online course (free) https://clicktosave.com.au/log-in/
- Free First Aid information https://bit.ly/2uvWOEJ and https://bit.ly/2G8Z8rl

Memberships and associations

- Melissa's Natural Healer Society https://naturalhealer.com.au/product/natural-healer-society-membership/

- Massage Association of Australia, for massage therapists in Australia https://www.maa.org.au/ (tell them I sent you so they look after you!)
- International Natural Healers Association https://www.internationalhealers.com/ (tell them I sent you so they look after you!)

Insurance

If you reach out to any of the insurers below, please tell them I sent you so they look after you!

- **Australia** – Insurance House https://bit.ly/2XjgsOL (Melissa's insurer)
- **USA** – Beauty & Bodywork Insurance http://bit.ly/2NdxUD9 (Melissa's preferred USA partner)
- **UK** – Protectivity Insurance https://bit.ly/2ClUmSM
- **Worldwide** – For insurance in all other countries, just do an internet search for "energy healing insurance" or "natural therapy insurance" and your country name. Then look for sites who you can find reviews for and compare from there.

Accountants and book keeping

Remember, your accountant should be one of the most consulted people in your contact list! So make sure you find a good one to partner up with!

- **Australia** – Finding a good accountant https://bit.ly/2E7VRUI
- **USA** – Finding a good accountant https://bit.ly/2u2YsLc
- **UK** – Finding a good accountant https://bit.ly/2xdP2OO
- **Worldwide** – Finding a good accountant https://bit.ly/2HpcDD9

Online book keeping tools

- Xero https://www.xero.com
- Quickbooks https://quickbooks.intuit.com

Business names and registration

Australia

- Check name availability https://bit.ly/2HuquXP
- Register https://register.business.gov.au/ or https://asic.gov.au/
- Trademark https://www.trademarkings.com.au/ (tell them I sent you so they look after you!)

USA

- Check name availability: https://bit.ly/2IrPAo7
- Register https://www.usa.gov/start-business
- Trademark https://www.uspto.gov/trademark

UK

- More information on how to set up and register https://www.gov.uk/set-up-business
- Trademark https://bit.ly/1wjddri

Worldwide

- For all other countries, if your accountant isn't going to do this for you, do an internet search for "how to start a business" and your country name. Then look for government sites, which usually have .gov in there somewhere.

Websites

You don't have to be "tech savvy" to start a website on any of the below platforms! They're relatively easy to set up and are large enough companies to be able to provide any support you need!

- Godaddy https://bit.ly/2wOMdVA
- Shopify https://www.shopify.com.au/

- Squarespace https://www.squarespace.com/
- Weebly https://www.weebly.com
- Wix https://www.wix.com/

Other platforms in place of a website

If you're not ready to launch your own website yet, here are some other platforms that are okay replacements for now. Just keep in mind though, *not* having an 'official' website doesn't appear as professional to potential clients.

- Facebook https://www.facebook.com/
- Setmore https://www.setmore.com/?ref=melissacrowhurst
- Simply Book Me https://simplybook.me/?ref=ida_2616
- Ebay (for 'physical' product sales) https://www.ebay.com/
- Etsy (for product sales) https://www.etsy.com/
- Zazzle (for product sales) https://www.zazzle.com

Popular social media platforms
- Facebook https://www.facebook.com/
- Instagram https://www.instagram.com
- Twitter https://twitter.com
- Pinterest https://www.pinterest.com
- Linkedin https://linkedin.com

Marketing tools

Training
- SEO training https://bit.ly/1zMwfYS
- Google Ads training https://bit.ly/2TBgFyt or https://youtu.be/cOTMWqwUXPU
- Facebook, Instagram, Messenger, and Whatsapp training https://bit.ly/2zo28Kp
- Email marketing https://bit.ly/2Fp7PvL

- *Ultimate Guide to Google AdWords: How to Access 100 Million People in 10 Minutes (Ultimate Series)* - Perry Marshall (Book) https://amzn.to/2UE1uRx
- *Ultimate Guide to Facebook Advertising: How to Access 1 Billion Potential Customers in 10 Minutes (Ultimate Series)* - Perry Marshall (Book) https://amzn.to/2FcnL3H
- *Instagram Secrets: The Underground Playbook for Growing Your Following Fast, Driving Massive Traffic & Generating Predictable Profits* - Jeremy McGilvrey (Book) https://amzn.to/2FcM6Gz

Advertising platforms
- Google Ads platform https://ads.google.com
- Facebook Ads https://www.facebook.com/business/ads
- Instagram Ads https://business.instagram.com/advertising/

Email marketing platforms
- Mailchimp https://mailchimp.com/
- Optin Monster https://optinmonster.com/
- Zoho https://www.zoho.com

Booking platforms
- Setmore: https://www.setmore.com/?ref=melissacrowhurst
- Simply Book Me https://simplybook.me/?ref=ida_2616

Client intake form
- Melissa's energy healing intake form: https://bit.ly/2SgjuQe

Payment gateways
Look into all of the below in order to easily accept payments online – which will easily integrate with many of the leading website platforms.

- Paypal https://www.paypal.com
- Stripe https://stripe.com
- Amazon Payments https://pay.amazon.com/us

Business Coaching

I personally know how overwhelming it can be to operate a successful business, and sometimes you need that little bit of help to get focused or back on track.

If you have questions or need more help, whether it's brainstorming your business ideas, trying to improve margins or efficiency, strategic marketing or growth planning, or perhaps something else – getting an outside perspective from an experienced business coach can make all the difference!

As such, I offer a very limited number of business coaching sessions (conducted online, via video conference) for my clients and students. You can learn more here: https://naturalhealer.com.au/product/business-coaching-session/

About the author

Melissa has over 25 years of entrepreneurial and business experience. Starting from publishing her own music magazine in her teens, to co-owning and operating a beauty salon with her mother, to conceptualizing, opening and quickly growing (and franchised!) a retail business with her husband Shawn in Australia.

Melissa also embarked on a journey of self-discovery once her and Shawn's business ventures were well underway, which lead to a very rewarding and beautiful spiritual awakening.

She has since mastered the healing arts of massage, Reiki, and meditation; sharpened her intuitive skills and awareness; as well as created her own 'spin' on healing, which she refers to as "loving energy healing" – you'll often see her hashtag it as #biglove!

Melissa is now the founder of Natural Healer where, as a Usui Reiki Master Teacher (2014) and Practitioner, Registered Natural Healer, Certified Meditation Teacher, Business Coach and Consultant, she offers online helps and courses that help blossom the soul.

She is also an author, podcaster, blogger, and speaker who loves sharing easy, actionable ways for people to heal themselves and others.

Deeming herself as an 'everyday' person, Melissa enjoys spending time with friends and family, loves a good laugh, adores animals, gets excited about cooking creative vegetarian meals, and delights in sharing life experiences with her husband Shawn.

Stay connected with Melissa!

Subscribe to Melissa's Blog

https://naturalhealer.com.au/blog/

Facebook

https://www.facebook.com/naturalhealerau

YouTube

https://www.youtube.com/c/NaturalhealerAu

ITunes

https://itunes.apple.com/au/podcast/natural-healer/id1133780594?mt=2

Twitter

https://twitter.com/naturalhealerau

Instagram

https://www.instagram.com/naturalhealerau/

Made in the USA
Monee, IL
04 June 2020